TeeJay

Mathematics

Curriculum for Excellence

Second Level
Book 2B

Written by the TeeJay Writing Group

HODDER GIBSON
AN HACHETTE UK COMPANY

Hachette UK's policy is to use papers that are natural, renewable and recyclable products and made from wood grown in well-managed forests and other controlled sources. The logging and manufacturing processes are expected to conform to the environmental regulations of the country of origin.

Orders

Please contact Bookpoint Ltd, 130 Park Drive, Milton Park, Abingdon, Oxon OX14 4SE. Telephone: (44) 01235 827827. Fax: (44) 01235 400401.

Email: education@bookpoint.co.uk

Lines are open from 9 a.m. to 5 p.m., Monday to Friday, with a 24-hour message answering service. You can also order through our website:

www.hoddergibson.co.uk

If you have queries or questions that aren't about an order you can contact us at hoddergibson@hodder.co.uk

We are an approved supplier on the Scotland Excel framework.

Schools can find us on their procurement system as: **TeeJay Publishers.**

The legal bit
© Hodder & Stoughton Ltd 2020
First published in 2020 by
TeeJay Publishers, an imprint of Hodder Gibson, which is part of the Hodder Education Group.
An Hachette UK Company
211 St Vincent Street
Glasgow, G2 5QY

www.hoddergibson.co.uk

Impression number 10 9 8 7 6 5 4 3 2
Year   2024 2023 2022 2021 2020

Printed in India

A catalogue record for this title is available from the British Library.

ISBN: 978 1 9077 8945 8

Second Level Book 2B

This book, along with CfE Book 2A, can be used in both Primary and Secondary with pupils who have successfully completed CfE First Level.

- Most pupils will complete the contents of Books 2A and 2B throughout Primary 5 to 7, some earlier and some later into Secondary 1 or 2. As a guide, Book 2B might be started with the majority of pupils at the beginning of, or part way through P6.

- There are no A and B exercises. The two books cover the entire Second Level CfE course without the teacher having to pick and choose which questions to leave out and which exercises are important. They all are!

- Pupils who cope well with the contents of Second Level may be able to begin work on Third Level during P7. Books 3A and 3B can then be used to work through CfE Third Level either at this stage or in Secondary 1 or 2.

- Book 2B, unlike Book 2A does not contain a "Chapter Zero". Instead, every chapter is preceded by a "Consolidation Exercise" which revises the corresponding work from Book 2A, prior to tackling the new work in the following chapter.

- Non-calculator skills are emphasised and encouraged throughout the book.

- Each chapter will have a "Revisit - Review - Revise" exercise as a summary. Answers for these can be found at www.hoddergibson.co.uk/answers-teejay-maths-2B

- Teachers are encouraged, at the end of various chapters, to consider assessing the pupils using the corresponding TeeJay Outcome Assessment.

- Homework* is available as a photocopiable pack.

- TeeJay's Assessment Pack* for each Level, early to Third, is available and can be used topic by topic or combined to form a series of Second Level cumulative Tests.

Pupils should then be able to complete their National 4/5 course leisurely by the end of S3 or early in S4.

We make no apologies for the multiplicity of colours used throughout the book, both for text and in diagrams - we feel it helps brighten up the pages !!

T Strang, J Geddes, J Cairns

(November 2011)

* Available for purchase separately.

Contents

Consolidation of Whole Numbers

1. Write out fully in words :- a 20 060   b 702 005

2. Write these numbers using digits :-

   a   twenty thousand eight hundred and thirty   b   sixty five thousand and four.

3. Rearrange the numbers given below in order, starting with the smallest :-

   29 028   29 208   30 002   28 982   30 010   28 899.

4. a   What numbers are represented by A, B, C and D on the given scales ?

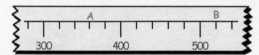 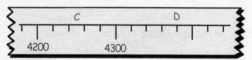

   b   What is the reading on this thermometer ?

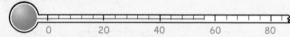

5. What number lies halfway between :-

   a   2900 and 3100   b   68 000 and 74 000 ?

6. Do the following mentally :-

   a   69 + 22   b   257 + 49   c   3200 + 4500   d   81 – 17

   e   2000 – 380   f   20 000 – 17 300 g   9999 + 12 400   h   9000 – 13.

7. Try this question mentally :-

   James empties his right pocket and finds he has 68p.

   He looks in his left pocket and discovers an extra 9p.

   He goes into a shop and spends 23p on a sweet.

   On the way home he finds a 50p coin on the ground.

   How much does James now have altogether ?

8. Set down the following and calculate :-

   a   5263   b   7529   c   6809 + 574   d   20 000 – 15 482.
     + 1638   – 3845

9. Round to the nearest 10 :-   a   68   b   584   c   3997.

10. Round to the nearest 100 :-   a   1239   b   6953   c   56 850.

11. Round to 1 figure accuracy and find an approximate answer to each of the following :-

    a   93 + 79   b   821 – 196   c   6820 + 2239   d   34 200 – 19 040.

12. Find :-

   a   53
       × 6

   b   8217
       × 7

   c   607 × 8

   d   5 × 2143.

13. Copy the following and complete :-

   a   9 ⟌ 504

   b   7132 ÷ 4

   c $\dfrac{6935}{5}$

   d   4312 ÷ 8.

14. Do the following mentally :-

   a   47 × 10

   b   10 × 2310

   c   504 × 100

   d   100 × 600

   e   9700 ÷ 10

   f   8000 ÷ 10

   g   49 000 ÷ 100

   h   16 000 ÷ 1000.

15. Attempt these problems, showing all working :-

   a   By 1950, 3279 species of butterflies had been discovered.
       During the following 50 years a further 1964 species
       were discovered.

       How many species of butterflies had been discovered altogether by 2000 ?

   b      A van driver makes a round trip of 243 km each day.

       How far does he drive working Monday to Saturday ?

   c   The combined weekly earnings of 5 office workers is £2085.

       If they get paid equally, how much does each earn ?

   d   Brian's hot tub holds 2615 litres. Davy's holds 1862 litres.

       How much more does Brian's hot tub hold than Davy's ?

   e   A small bag of cement weighs 23 kg. A truck is loaded with 100 bags.

       If the empty truck weighs 215 kg, what is the total weight of
       the truck and the bags of cement ?

16. Do the following :-

   a   203 × 4 × 7

   b   1890 ÷ 7 ÷ 5.

17. Put the correct sign (+, −, ×, ÷) into the calculations to make the statements correct :-

   a   27 ◯ 27 = 54   b   91 ◯ 91 = 0   c   15 ◯ 15 = 225   d   63 ◯ 63 = 1.

18. Explain a simple rule for multiplying a number by a million.

Chapter 1

Place Values

Understand place value for numbers up to 1 000 000 and beyond

Example :-

In the number 2 346 785,

the 2 stands for two million	2 000 000
the 3 stands for three hundred thousand	300 000
the 4 stands for forty thousand	40 000
the 6 stands for six thousand	6 000
the 7 stands for seven hundred	700
the 8 stands for eight tens	80
the 5 stands for five units	5
	2 346 785

Two million, three hundred and forty six thousand, seven hundred and eighty five.

2 346 785 ✓

Exercise 1

1. What do the following digits stand for in the number 1 487 293 :-

   a 1   b 7   c 8   d 4   e 9 ?

2. What does the 7 stand for in each of these numbers :-

   a 58 740   b 35 279   c 647 900   d 7 340 601 ?

3. Write the following numbers out fully in words :-

   a 4080   b 21 900   c 71 350   d 235 080

   e 703 460   f 1 870 000 g 4 093 070   h 27 050 062.

4. Write the following numbers using digits :-

   a four thousand, two hundred and nine   b seventeen thousand and fifty

   c sixty thousand and ninety eight   d two hundred and thirty thousand and one

   e five million, four hundred and seven thousand

   f one million and seven

   g twelve million, sixty thousand and forty.

5. Put the following sets of numbers in order, smallest first :-

   a 7068, 6876, 7086, 6786, 7008, 7080, 6867.

   b 100 870, 99 924, 100 086, 98 999, 90 887, 100 076.

6. Write down the number that is :-

   a 40 after 290   b 200 after 1990   c 70 before 394 210

   d 600 before 11 450   e 4000 after 269 001   f 1500 before 600 000

   g 8700 after 975 000   h 200 500 before 3 300 500.

7. Look at the following scales. What numbers are represented by the letters **A**, **B**, **C**, ... ?

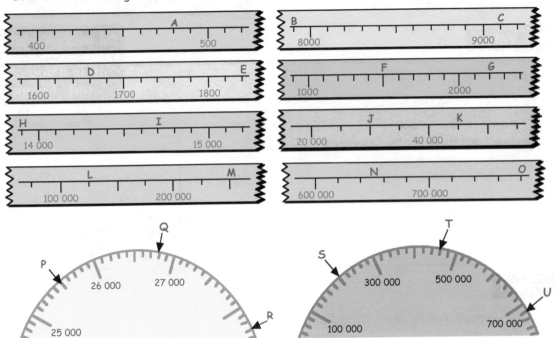

8. What number lies **halfway** between :-

   a   970 and 980

   b   3400 and 3500

   c   44 000 and 44 700

   d   820 000 and 880 000

   e   730 500 and 830 500

   f   940 000 and 1 200 000 ?

9. Write out in figures :-

   a   1 million
   b $\frac{1}{2}$ million
   c $\frac{1}{4}$ million
   d $\frac{3}{4}$ million.

10. In July 2011, a family from Largs won £161·653 million in the Eurolottery.
    That was the largest amount ever won since it started.

    a   Write out this amount of money in full, **in figures**.

    b   Now write it out, **using words**.

11.

    Chelsea paid £2·3 million for a defender.
    Liverpool paid £6·5 million for a forward.

    Arsenal paid exactly **halfway** between these payments for a goalkeeper.

    Write how much Arsenal paid, **in words**.

12. a   By the late 2010's, the population of China is expected to reach 1·4 billion.

       Write out this number fully, **in figures**.

    b   Find the population of 6 other countries and write them **in figures**.

Be able to multiply and divide by 30, 200, 4000 etc.

To multiply by 30, 200 or 4000, use two steps :-

    Step 1   =>   multiply by the 10, 100 or 1000 first

    Step 2   =>   then multiply by the 3, 2, 4 etc.

Examples :-

To multiply 382×30

Step 1   Find $382 \times 10 = 3820$

Step 2   Find 3820×3 ...

$$\begin{array}{r} 3820 \\ \times\ 3 \\ \hline 11\,460 \end{array}$$

To multiply 218×400

Step 1   Find $218 \times 100 = 21\,800$

Step 2   Find $21\,800 \times 4$ ...

$$\begin{array}{r} 21\,800 \\ \times\ 4 \\ \hline 87\,200 \end{array}$$

Exercise 2

1.   Try to do the following **mentally** :-   (*use the 2-step approach*)

    a 17×20 b 42×30 c 19×60

    d 33×50 e 40×223 f 70×204

    g 61×200 h 400×34 i 115×600

    j 800×212 k 2000×24 l 130×9000.

2.   Calculate each of the following (*not necessarily mentally*) :-

    a 436×30 [Find 436×10 first $= 436\underline{0}$ and then find 4360×3]

    b 617×40 c 209×50 d 3218×60

    e 70×980 f 1231×80 g 6507×90

    h 2184×30 i 90×3046 j $12\,345 \times 20$.

3.   Work out each of the following using the same 2 steps :-

    a 108×400 [Find 304×100 first $= 30\,400$ and then find $30\,400 \times 3$]

    b 352×300 c 456×500 d 179×700

    e 758×200 f 600×305 g 975×300

    h 407×800 i 900×821 j 2000×732

    k 706×6000 l 452×4000 m 734×3000

    n 8000×119 o 7000×2043 p 9000×5320.

There is a quick way of doing the following multiplications mentally :-

Example :- 40 000 x 8000

=> simply find 4 x 8 (= 32) and then add on 7 zeros => 320 000 000

4. Do the following mentally :-

a 60 x 20

b 80 x 90

c 700 x 40

d 500 x 90

e 50 x 7000

f 80 x 600

g 200 x 900

h 500 x 900

i 3000 x 700

j 600 x 9000

k 4000 x 7000

l 6000 x 8000.

Similarly, there is a quick way of doing the following divisions mentally :-

Example :- 420 000 ÷ 6000

=> simply cancel out equal numbers of zeros 420 000 ÷ 6000

=> then do the simpler division 420 ÷ 6 = 70.

5. Do the following mentally :-

a 2100 ÷ 30

b 2800 ÷ 40

c 49 000 ÷ 70

d 24 000 ÷ 400

e 180 000 ÷ 3000

f 600 000 ÷ 200

g 5 600 000 ÷ 800

h 25 500 000 ÷ 500

i 4 200 000 ÷ 600

j 4 160 000 ÷ 8000

k 21 700 000 ÷ 7000

l 5 670 000 ÷ 9000.

6. a 20 cars in a garage forecourt had each done 38 000 miles.

What is the combined number of miles these cars have travelled ?

b

A machine automatically puts chewy sweets into jars. 7500 chews are spread equally into 60 jars.

How many are in each jar ?

c 300 workers in a telesales company are in a lottery syndicate. They win the second prize of £417 000.

How much should each person receive ?

d

There are 1440 minutes in 1 day.

How many minutes are there in 50 days ?

7. When you write all the numbers from 1 to 20 :-

1, 2, 3, 4, 5, 6, 7, 8, 9, 10, 11, 12, 13, 14, 15, 16, 17, 18, 19, 20

you will have used 31 digits altogether.

How many digits are needed to write all the numbers from :-

a 1 to 100

b 1 to 1000

c 1 to 1 000 000 ?

Rounding to nearest 10, 100 and 1000

Revision :-

To round to the nearest 10   look at the units digit :-

- if it is a 0, 1, 2, 3 or 4 -   leave the 10's digit as it is.
- if it is a 5, 6, 7, 8 or 9 -   round the 10's digit up by one.

157 —> 160

To round to the nearest 100   look at the tens digit :-

- if it is a 0, 1, 2, 3 or 4 -   leave the 100's digit as it is.
- if it is a 5, 6, 7, 8 or 9 -   round the 100's digit up by one.

2374 —> 2400

To round to the nearest 1000   look at the units digit :-

- if it is a 0, 1, 2, 3 or 4 -   leave the 1000's digit as it is.
- if it is a 5, 6, 7, 8 or 9 -   round the 1000's digit up by one.

18 497 —> 18 000

Exercise 3

1. Round to the nearest 10 :-

   a   57   b   42   c   69   d   35   e   18
   f   183   g   375   h   292   i   8   j   405
   k   594   l   329   m   2766   n   9804   o   7096.

2. Round to the nearest 100 :-

   a   332   b   872   c   829   d   784   e   250
   f   777   g   4747   h   4098   i   9480   j   7241
   k   26 284 l   29 850 m   16 050 n   7891   o   20 495.

3. Round to the nearest 1000 :-

   a   8700   b   23 200 c   48 810 d   37 960 e   57 482
   f   91 501 g   19 610 h   77 499 i   83 960 j   74 498
   k   16 505 l   357 600 m   436 492 n   368 602 o   799 984.

4.   The overall attendance at Wimbledon 2011 was 489 946.

   Round this figure to the nearest :-

   a   10   b   100   c   1000.

5. At the time of his signing for Chelsea, Michael Essien was the most expensive African footballer in history. He cost £24 356 000.

   Round this figure to the nearest :-

   a   £10 000   b   £million   c   £10 million.

Using Rounding to Estimate Answers

Make sure you know your tables!

Use rounding to simplify the estimation of the answer to a question

It is possible to "MENTALLY" estimate the answer to a question by rounding the numbers to "1 figure" accuracy first.

Examples :-

$$79 \times 42$$
is approximately
$$80 \times 40$$
$$\approx 3200$$

$$7982 \div 396$$
is approximately
$$8000 \div 400$$
$$\approx 20$$

"≈" approximately equal to.

Exercise 4

1. The answer to 62×78 is either {486, 4836 or 48 036}. (no calculator !)

   By rounding $62 \times 78 = 60 \times$ ..... = ... , decide which of the 3 answers has to be the correct one.

2. Round your numbers before multiplying. Use this to decide which of the 3 given answers is most likely to be the correct one :-

   a 39×61 Choice of   {237·9,   2379   or   23 799}

   b 178×18 Choice of   {3204,   32 440   or   32 004}

   c 614×57 Choice of   {3498,   34 998   or   349 908}

   d 293×116 Choice of   {5849,   13 988,   or   33 988}

   e $153 832 \div 287$ Choice of   {53 600,   5360   or   536}

3. Round each number to 1 figure accuracy, then give an estimate for :-

   a 71×28 b 37×52 c 88×81 d 397×61

   e 304×78 f 785×182 g $796 \div 16$ h $4031 \div 37$

   i $5918 \div 192$ j $64 128 \div 302$ k $19 096 \div 188$ l $99 909 \div 2347$.

4. a   A tin of pea & ham soup weighs 415 grams.

      What is the approximate weight of a box containing 36 tins ?

   b   A school put in a £110 624 bid to the Council for 208 laptops.

      Approximately, what was the cost of a laptop ?

   c   On average, a coach driver travels 37 918 miles per year while at work.

      If a bus company employs 175 drivers, what will the approximate total milage travelled by these drivers be ?

Using a Calculator

Exercise 5

 ✓

Solve problems involving +, -, ×, ÷ using a calculator when needed

1. A supermarket buyer bought 3500 litres of cola at 80p per litre.

   What did she pay for all this juice ?

2.  Tennis player Rory McGrory has earned £1·25 million so far in his career. Angus McTavish has so far won £785 000 in prize money.

   How much is Rory ahead of Angus in winnings ?

3. A chief executive earns a gross yearly salary of £1 357 180. His total **deductions** for tax etc. come to £271 436, which is taken off his gross salary.

   How much money is he left with in his pay ?

4. A Secondary Teejay Maths Textbook has 106 double sided pages.

   How many pages are needed to print :-

   a   500 books   b   14 000 books ?

5. The attendances for 3 rugby matches at kick-off time are shown.

   a   How many spectators were present in total at the start of the matches ?

   b   If a total of 16 892 spectators left the games before they finished how many were still in the stadia at the end ?

Accies	14 123
Warriors	12 371
Rovers	10 729

6. A notepad has 280 sheets of paper.

   How many sheets are there in 36 notepads ?

7. A shop has three thousand seven hundred and eighty DVD's to sell.

   If an equal amount are stacked on to twelve shelves, how many DVD's are on each shelf ?

8. Betty gets paid £15 per hour and worked 42 hours last week. Her husband Joe gets paid £13 per hour and worked 39 hours last week.

   How much did they earn **altogether** ?

9. A greengrocer bought 30 boxes of oranges for £482. He sold them for £18 per box.

   a   How much money did he collect when he sold all the boxes of oranges ?

   b   How much more was this than he had paid for them ?

10. When full, London's Dominion Theatre holds 2100 people.

If the theatre was full 250 nights in a row, how many people visited it ?

11. A group of 80 part-time telesales operators took 5120 calls in total in one hour.

Assuming they are scheduled to take the same number of calls, how many calls did each operator take in the hour ?

12. The Greig family won £159 300 in the Lottery.
Each got an equal share of £13 275.

How many people must there be in the Greig family ?

13. Paris spends £180 every time she visits the beauty parlour. She goes there every two months, knowing she has to stick to a budget of £1000 a year.

Does Paris stick to her budget ? Explain.

14. A Boeing 777 can carry 430 passengers.

How many of these planes are needed to take 7740 football supporters to a Champions League away match ?

15.  In a new housing estate all 170 houses are identical. A total of 400 180 bricks were used to build them.

How many bricks were used for each house ?

16. A box holds 375 envelopes. A car insurance company orders 25 boxes. 8950 envelopes are used to send information about their new product to customers.

How many envelopes does the company have left ?

17.  Thomas had a conservatory built in August 2011.
It cost £16 800 plus tax at £3360.

a   What was the total cost of his conservatory at this point ?

Thomas received a voucher from the company for £275 for introducing a friend.

b   What was the final cost of the conservatory to Thomas ?

18. Film star Jan Ravolta cannot get used to her fame.
She buys a private jet by paying £575 000. She then made
20 monthly payments of £230 000 to complete her purchase.

What is the total cost of her plane ?

19. Jenny bought 1160 euros for £800 in a bank.
Her brother got 1776 euros for £1200 from a travel agent.

a   Work out how many euros each of them received for £1.

b   Who got the better buy ?

BOMDAS - the Order of Operations

Be able to
+, -, ×, ÷
using the order
of operations

Many calculations have to be completed in a specific order.

(You will find out much later in Mathematics why !)

Example :- For 3 + 4 x 2 .... the answer is NOT .. 7 x 2 = 14. The answer IS ...... 3 + 8 = 11.

An easy way to remember which part of a calculation comes first is using the mnemonic BOMDAS.

Example 1

5 + 3 x 2

Multiply first

= 5 + 6

= 11

Example 2

one half of 30 ÷ 5

Of first

= 15 ÷ 5

= 3

Example 3

(18 − 2) ÷ (2 x 4)

Brackets first

= 16 ÷ 8

= 2

· Multiply & Divide rank equally
· Add & Subtract rank equally

1	2	3	4
B	O	M or D	A or S

After you have done any B(rackets) or O(f), then go from left to right doing any M(ultiplication) or D(ivision) as you find them. Then go from left to right doing any A(ddition) or S(ubtraction) as you find them.

Exercise 6

Brackets
Of
Multiplication
Division
Addition
Subtraction

1. Use BOMDAS to help you calculate :-

   a   10 + 7 x 2   b   11 + 2 x 3   c   3 x 2 + 6

   d   20 − 16 ÷ 4   e   60 − 50 ÷ 10   f   13 − 12 ÷ 2.

2. Calculate :-

   a   20 − 12 + 2 − 10   b   quarter of 20 ÷ 5   c   fifth of 50 − 10

   d $\frac{1}{2}$ of 16 ÷ 4   e   10 + $\frac{1}{3}$ of 15   f   13 − $\frac{1}{4}$ of 12 + 2

   g   5 x 3 − 12 ÷ 4 + 8   h   5 x 4 − 2 x 3 + 16 ÷ 4   i   13 − $\frac{1}{4}$ of (20 − 8).

3. Find, showing two more steps each time :-

   a   5 + (12 ÷ 2)   b   16 ÷ (10 − 2)   c   5 x (6 + 3)

   d   100 ÷ (6 + 4)   e   6 x (7 + 2) − 24   f   (5 + 2) x (6 − 2) + 5.

4. Find :-

   a   100 ÷ 4 + 5 x 2   b   a quarter of (16 + 4)   c   6 x (5 + 4)

   d   6 x 5 + 4   e   6 + 5 x 4   f   (6 + 5) x 4

   g   100 − $\frac{1}{2}$ of 10 x 10   h $\frac{1}{2}$ of ($\frac{1}{3}$ of 12)   i   ((6 + 4) + 2) x 3 − (20 + 2).

5. Copy each of the following and insert brackets to make each calculation correct :-

   a   5 + 3 x 2 = 16   b   18 − 5 x 2 = 8   c   20 + 4 ÷ 6 = 4

   d   10 + 6 ÷ 2 x 5 = 25   e   10 + 20 ÷ 5 − 1 = 15   f   5 + 2 x 8 − 6 ÷ 2 = 7.

Revisit - Review - Revise

1. a   Round to the nearest 10 :-   (i) 88   (ii) 3694   (iii) 12 747
    b   Round to the nearest 100 :-   (i) 346   (ii) 1480   (iii) 17 382
    c   Round to the nearest 1000 :-   (i) 5548   (ii) 29 672   (iii) 328 299.

2. a   Round both numbers to the nearest 10, then estimate :-   369 + 385
    b   Round both numbers to the nearest 100, then estimate :-   7452 – 1718
    c   Round both numbers to the nearest 1000, then estimate :-   17 840 + 6499.

3. Estimate :-   a   3164 x 9   b   17 868 ÷ 6.

4. Cheryl bought two second hand cars - a classic
    at £4356 and a convertible costing £3842.

    Round both these prices to the nearest £100
    and find an approximate answer for the total
    amount she paid for the cars.

5.    West Fife signed Davie Prunty for £28 625 and Jamie
    Greig for £19 365.

    Round both figures to the nearest £1000 and find out
    approximately how much more expensive Prunty was
    than Greig.

6. The population of Scotland in the autumn of 2010 was 5 252 100.

    Round this number to the nearest hundred thousand.

7. Set down these calculations and work them out :-
    a   17 586 + 312   b   48 104 – 37 889   c   1874 x 7
    d   3679 x 4   e   38 429 + 122 485   f   12 976 x 9
    g   129 705 ÷ 5   h   26 307 ÷ 3   i   2 834 312 ÷ 8.

8. Write down the answer to :-
    a   430 x 10   b   367 x 1000   c   458 x 100   d   6000 x 1000
    e   270 ÷ 10   f   23 900 ÷ 100   g   7 804 000 ÷ 100 h   7 102 000 ÷ 1000.

9. Find :-
    a   145 x 30   b   74 x 200   c   599 x 500   d   123 x 8000
    e   540 ÷ 60   f   23 800 ÷ 700   g   7 804 800 ÷ 900 h   7 160 000 ÷ 4000.

10. I flew from Aberdeen to New York, a distance of 3280 miles and then on to Los Angeles, a further 2448 miles.

    a   How far did I travel in total ?

    b   How much longer was the first journey ?

Los Angeles Airport

11. When a number is multiplied by 9 the answer is 78 714.

    What is that number ?

12.    700 metres of plastic piping costs £2030 to lay.

    600 metres of metal piping is priced £1800 to lay.

    a   Calculate the cost of one metre of piping for each.

    b   Which is the cheaper piping to put down ?

13. The total amount of annual fees collected by the secretary of a golf club consisting of 480 members was £397 200.

    How much did each member have to pay ?

14.    There are 48 tins of tomato soup in a carton.
    There are 20 cartons in a box.
    There are 15 boxes in a crate and 8 crates on a lorry.

    How many tins of soup are on the lorry ?

15. 35 people work a six hour shift at a call centre.

    If the total wage bill for them is £1470, what is their hourly rate of pay ?

16.    A buyer for a phone store bought 60 phones for £2280.

    The store managed to sell all but 5 of them for £42 each.

    a   How much money did the store take in ?

    b   How much did the store make out of these sales ?

17. Gerri bought a new people carrier worth £35 620. She arranged to pay the garage £7 000 and then pay what was still owed over a period of 36 months.

    After that first payment :-

    a   how much did she still owe the garage ?

    b   what had she to pay per month to clear what she owed ?

Consolidation of Symmetry

1. Define, in your own words, what is meant by saying that a shape has a line of symmetry.

2. How many lines of symmetry do each of the following shapes have ?

   a    b   c   d

   e    f   g   h

3. Trace or copy these shapes NEATLY onto squared paper.

   a    b 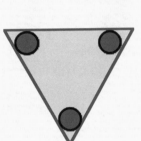   c

   Mark in colour ALL the lines of symmetry.

4. Trace or copy the following shapes neatly and draw in the other half so the red lines are lines of symmetry.

   a 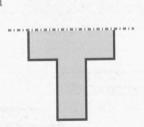   b    c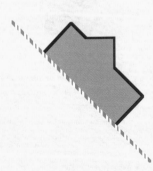

Chapter 2

Creating a Symmetrical Shape

Be able to create "the other half" of a symmetrical shape

If you are given half of a symmetrical shape on a grid with the line of symmetry shown, it is fairly straightforward to create the other half.

Example :-

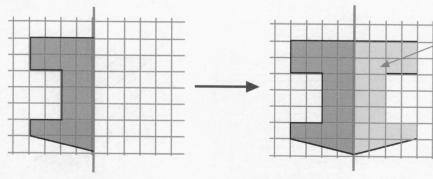

the "other half"

Discuss different ways of creating the above symmetrical shape.

Exercise 1   (You will need a ruler)

1. a   Copy this shape onto squared paper.
      (*or into your jotter*).

   b   Now draw in and shade/colour the other half such that the green line is a line of symmetry.

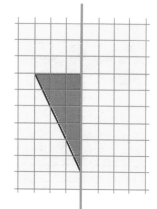

2. Copy each of the following shapes neatly onto squared paper, then complete each shape so that the green line is a line of symmetry.

a 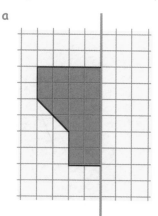   b 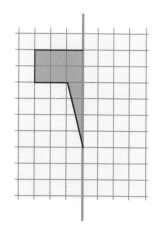   c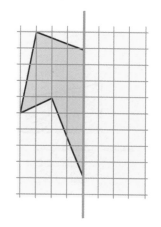

2. d 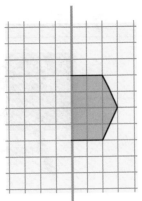   e 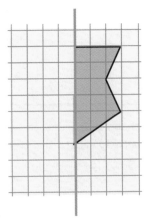   f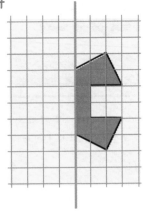

g 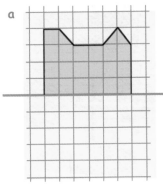   h 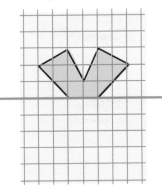   i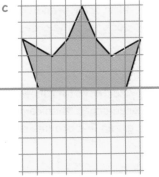

3. Copy each of the following shapes neatly onto squared paper, then complete each shape so that the green line is a line of symmetry.

a 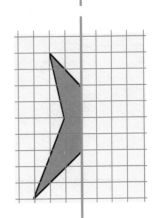   b    c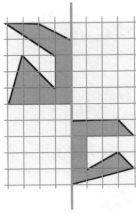

d 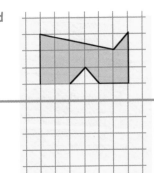   e 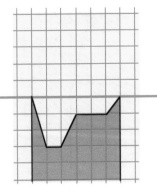   f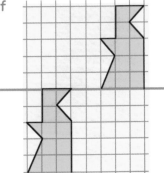

4. These are harder. Copy and draw the other half of the following symmetrical shapes :-

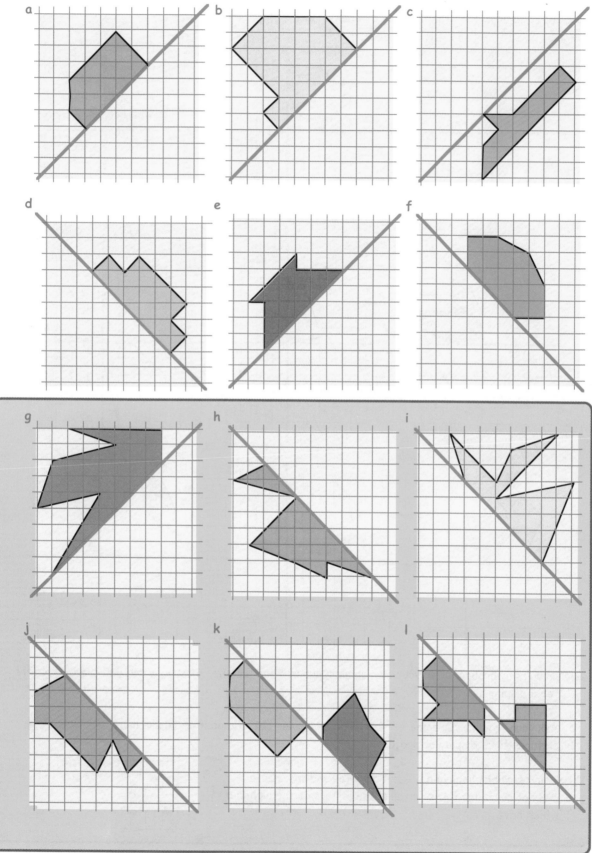

5. This time, each shape has 2 lines of symmetry, each shown in green.

Copy and draw the other 3 parts of each shape.

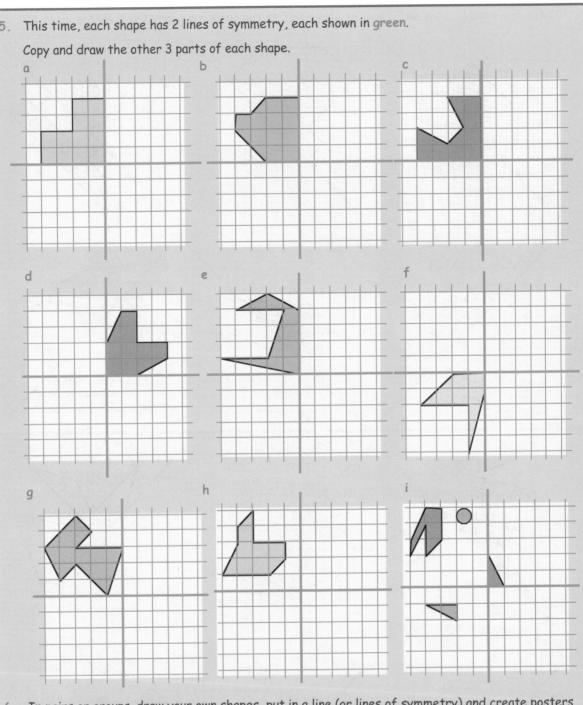

6. In pairs or groups, draw your own shapes, put in a line (or lines of symmetry) and create posters for a display.

7. Ask your teacher for some isometric or triangular dotted paper and make more symmetrical pictures for a display or project.

8. Using straight lines and a 4 x 4 grid, (as shown) create a set of computer fonts for all those letters of the alphabet which have exactly 1 line of symmetry.

Revisit - Review - Revise

1. Copy or trace each of these shapes and draw in any lines of symmetry :-

a

b

c

d

e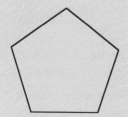

f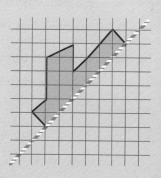

2. Complete each shape so that the dotted line is a line of symmetry :-

a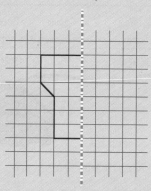

b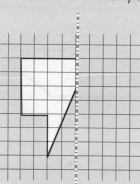

c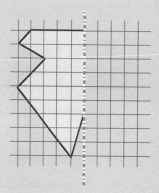

d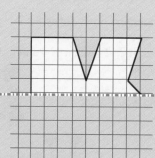

e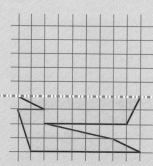

f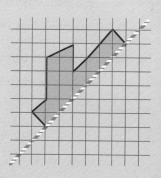

Consolidation of Time

1. Write the following in 12 hour format :- (remember to use am or pm).

   a 0302　　　b 1840　　　c 1038　　　d 2345.

2. Change these times to 24 hour format :-

   a 5.30 am　　b 5.02 pm　　c 20 to midnight　　d Noon

   e 1245 am　　f 5 to 10 at night　　g 10 past midnight　　h $\frac{1}{4}$ to 8 at night.

3. Jason left for school at 0815 and returned home at 1605.

   How long had he been away ?

4. The local postie started work at 20 to 7 in the morning.
   It took him 5 hours and 35 minutes to sort and deliver the mail .

   When did he finish his work ?

5. A bus is laid on twice per day to take shoppers from a country village to specialist shops in the area. The shoppers are allowed 20 minutes in each shop.

   A timetable showing DEPARTURE times from each shop is shown below.

	Village Centre	Mosco Market	Harry's Fish Shop	Irn Mongers	Holmes Farm	Cospo Homeware	Tea Shop
Bus 1	0925	1010	1040	1115	1135	1155	1220
Bus 2	1425	1445	1540				

   a When does the 1st bus arrive at Irn Mongers ?

   b How long does the journey from Harry's Fish to Irn Mongers take ?

   c How long does it take from leaving Holmes Farm to arriving at the Tea Shop ?

   d Assuming both buses go at the same speed, at what time will bus 2 leave the Tea Shop ?

6. a How many days are there in :-　　(i) April　　(ii) October ?

   b How many days from 25th of June and 10th of July, including both dates ?

7. May ran a half marathon in 2 hours and 12 minutes. Kate ran it in 1 hour and 48 minutes.

   a Who finished first and by how many minutes ?

   b If they ran a full marathon at the same pace how long would each take ?

8. Cyprus time is 2 hours ahead of British time.

   This means that when it is 9 am here, it is 11 am in Cyprus.

   I flew from Glasgow Airport to sunny Cyprus, leaving at 1020.

   If the flight took 5 hours 25 minutes, at what time (Cyprus time), did I arrive at Pathos Airport in Cyprus ?

Chapter 3

Longer Time Intervals

Be able to calculate a time interval

Counting on :-   As we saw in Book 2a, the easiest way of finding how long something lasts is by "counting on".

Example 1 :-

A late night film started at 2250 and lasted for 2 hours 15 minutes. When did it finish ?

$$2250 \xrightarrow{\text{+ 2 hours}} 2450 \ (0050) \xrightarrow{\text{+ 15 mins}} 0065 \ (= 0105) \longrightarrow \text{Finished at 0105 next day.}$$

Example 2 :-

How long is it from 7.05 pm on Friday until 1.30 pm on Saturday ?

$$7.05 \text{ pm} \overset{\text{55 mins}}{\frown} 8 \text{ pm} \overset{\text{+ 4 hours}}{\frown} \text{midnight} \overset{\text{+ 13 hours}}{\frown} 1 \text{ pm} \overset{\text{+ 30 mins}}{\frown} 1.30 \text{ pm} \overset{\text{= 17 hrs 85 mins}}{=} 18 \text{ hours 25 mins.}$$

Exercise 1

1. What time is it :-

   a   1 hour after 0730
   b   2 hours after 1850
   c   3 hours 30 minutes after 0930
   d   4 hours 5 minutes after 1555
   e   1 hour 30 minutes after 2330
   f   3 hours 40 minutes after 1745
   g   5 hours 50 minutes after 2130 Friday
   h   6 hours 45 minutes after 1920 Tuesday
   i   7 hours 8 minutes after 2032 Monday
   j   9 hours 22 minutes after 1848 Saturday ?

2. What time is it :-

   a   2 hours after 6.50 pm
   b   3 hours after 8.32 am
   c   4 hours 30 minutes after 8 am
   d   3 hours 25 minutes after 8 pm
   e   2 hours 45 minutes after 3.15 pm
   f   4 hours 20 minutes after 9.40 pm Monday
   g   6 hours 40 minutes after 9.10 am
   h   2 hours 50 minutes after 11.40 pm Thursday
   i   5 hours 50 minutes after 11.20 pm Fri.
   j   8 hours 20 minutes after 9.50 pm Wed. ?

3. What is the time :-

   a   1 hour before 2330
   b   2 hours before 9.32 pm
   c   1 hour 30 minutes before 0240
   d   3 hours 5 minutes before 1900
   e   3 hours 20 minutes before 6.30 am
   f   1 hour 30 minutes before 0030 Sunday
   g   3 hours 20 minutes before 2 am Tues.
   h   4 hours 45 minutes before 3.15 am Wed.
   i   6 hours 25 minutes after 1950 Mon.
   j   9 hours 15 minutes after 8.15 pm on Frid. ?

4. How long is it from :-

   a 4.15 pm to 10.15 pm

   b midnight to 2.30 pm

   c 8.45 am to 11.20 am

   d 1735 to 2130

   e 1315 to 2105

   f 9 am to 8.10 pm

   g 4.30 pm to 9.20 pm

   h 9 pm Wednesday to 1.30 am Thursday

   i 11.30 pm Monday to 3.15 am Tuesday

   j 2245 Saturday to 1045 Monday ?

5. These clocks indicate the start of the activities
   for a day at the U-IN-THE-PARK music
   festival and when they were due to end.

   For how long did the festival last that day ?

Start am → End pm

6. One bright morning Tommy decided to cycle to work. He left home at 0645.
   It took exactly 1 hour 18 minutes to get there.

   Did he make it to his office on time for an 8 am start ? (*Explain*).

7. Sammi plans to meet her pen pal in Paris at 9.40 am on the Sunday morning.
   She thinks that if she takes the overnight train, leaving Inverness at
   11.25 pm on the Saturday, she will have enough time to get to Paris.
   The journey from Inverness to Paris, via London, is to take 10 hours
   10 minutes.

   Will Sammi make it on time ?

8. Jet3's scheduled flight to Portugal leaves Edinburgh Airport
   every Tuesday and Friday at 2255.
   The flight takes 3 hours 17 minutes.

   What time are the flights due to land in Portugal ?

9. British Airways flight BA123 left Gatwick Airport at 1855 on Monday and
   arrived in Las Vegas at 0505 (British time) on Tuesday morning.

   a How long did the flight take ?

   b Las Vegas is 8 hours behind London time.

      What time was it in Las Vegas when the plane landed ?

10. How long is it from :-

    a 2230 on Wednesday 1st August until 2240 on Friday 3rd August

    b 2.45 pm on Monday 19th November until Thursday 22nd November at 3 pm

    c 2130 on Tuesday 10th February until 0010 on Thursday 12th February ?

More About Timetables

Exercise 2

1. Here are the train timetables for
    "London to Perth" and "Perth to London".

London	<—>	Perth			Perth	<—>	London		
London Euston	leave	0525	2115		Perth	leave	0910	1922	
Watford	arrive	0544	2133		Gleneagles	arrive	0930	1941	
	leave	0545	2134			leave	0932	1943	
Crewe		0805	2355		Dunblane		0945	1957	
Preston	arrive	0903	0052		Stirling	arrive	0956	2008	
	leave	0908	0057			leave	1000	2009	
Stirling		1323	0454		Preston		1415	0032	
Dunblane		1334	0504		Crewe		1514	0132	
Gleneagles	arrive	1349	0520		Watford	arrive	1730	0353	
	leave	1351	0522			leave	1732	0355	
Perth	arrive	1410	0541		London Euston	arrive	1749	0410	

Write the following times in **12 hour time with am or pm** :-

a   When did the overnight train from London to Perth leave Preston ?

b   At what time did the overnight train from Perth to London pass through Preston ?

c   At what times do the trains leave Watford for London ?

d   For how long do all trains stop at Gleneagles ?

e   On the daytime London to Perth train, how long is the journey from Stirling to Dunblane ?

f   On the daytime Perth to London train, how long is the journey from Dunblane to Stirling ?

g   On the overnight London to Perth train, how long is the journey from Preston to Stirling ?

h   On the overnight Perth to London train, how long is the journey from Stirling to Preston ?

i   You were hoping to board the London bound train at Stirling Station, but arrived 10
     minutes too late for the morning train. How long is it till the next one ?

j   I left London on the early train for a meeting in Gleneagles at 2.30 pm. The train pulls out
     of London 35 minutes late. Am I still likely to be on time for my meeting ?

k   Which of the four trains takes the shortest time between the two cities ?

Shown below is an extract from a advert for holidays from Glasgow Airport in 2011.

Flying To	Time	No. Days	Flying No.	Dates	Company
Malaga	Sun 0545	14	TAX4533	08/05-16/10	TourAir
Malaga	Sun 1315	7	DBX4534	08/05-16/10	Direct Breaks
Malta	Tue 0855	7 & 14	TAX3014	03/05-25/10	TourAir
Malta	Tue 0855	7	TAX3014	03/05-25/10	Direct Breaks
Naples	Fri 1455	7 & 14	FCX1544	06/05-28/08	First Class Hols
Naples	Fri 1455	7 & 14	FCX1544	06/08-28/10	Timmy Cook
Orlando	Mon 1005	14	TAX328	27/06-18/07	TourAir
Orlando	Fri 0430	14	DBX328	24/06-18/09	Direct Breaks
Majorca	Sat 1750	7	TCX1138	15/10-15/10	Timmy Cook
Majorca	Sat 2145	10	DBX1139	15/10-15/10	Direct Breaks

Malaga	Sun 0545	14	TAX4533	08/05-16/10	TourAir

Means that the holiday is in Malaga, Spain, leaving Glasgow on Sunday at 5.45 am for 14 days and the flight number is TAX4533. The holiday is available between 8th May - 16th October, flying with TourAir.

2. a   State all of the details for the Monday flight to Orlando.

   b   First Class Holidays only offer 1 holiday. Where to and for how long ?

   c   If I can only go to Orlando on a Friday, at what time is the flight (am/pm) and with which tour company ?

   d   I want to go for a 10 day break.

        Give the full details of my only choice.

   e   Sheila decides to go to Malaga for 7 days.

        When is her flight and what company must she book it with ?

   f   I want to go on holiday on 28th October. Where can I go and what's the flight number ?

   g   There are 2 flights to Majorca :-   (i)   what is the "same" about these flights ?

                                          (ii) list four "differences".

   h   List the two "differences" when comparing the flights to Malta.

   i   I leave on Sunday 8th May in the afternoon.
        Give the full details of this holiday.

3.   Use a computer or a holiday brochure to plan a holiday sometime in the near future to a hot country for 2 weeks for a family of four, 2 adults and two children aged 4 and 8.

   a   List all the details including the cost.

   b   Make a list of all the essential things needed for the holiday.

Minutes and Seconds   *Revision*

When adding or subtracting units of time you need to remember that there are 60 seconds in 1 minute.

Adding :-

	2 mins	20 secs
+	6 mins	50 secs
	9 mins	10 secs

70 secs = 1 min 10 secs

Subtracting :-

	6 mins	20 secs
−	2 mins	40 secs
	3 mins	40 secs

60 + 20 − 40 = 40 secs

Remember:-
1 hour = 60 minutes
1 minute = 60 seconds

Exercise 3

1. One of Elvis' Rock & Roll songs "Jailhouse Rock" lasts for 155 seconds.
    Write this time in **minutes** and **seconds**.

2. Change each of these to **minutes** and **seconds** :-

    a   80 secs
    b   138 secs
    c   210 secs
    d   300 secs
    e   930 secs
    f   600 secs.

3. Change each of these to **hours** and **minutes** :-

    a   95 mins
    b   135 mins
    c   255 mins
    d   480 mins
    e   1210 mins
    f   6000 mins.

4. Copy the following and complete :-

    a
	3 mins	10 secs
+	5 mins	45 secs

    b
	6 mins	40 secs
+	2 mins	40 secs

    c
	9 hrs	35 mins
+	2 hrs	45 mins

    d
	6 mins	35 secs
−	3 mins	20 secs

    e
	8 mins	00 secs
−	2 min	45 secs

    f
	9 hrs	30 mins
−	8 hrs	50 mins

5. Four men ran in a 4 by 1000 metre relay race. Their times were as follows :-
    Mike - 2 mins 45 secs, Alex - 2 mins 50 secs, Eric - 2 mins 25 secs, Bill - 2 mins 35 secs.
    How long did the race last **altogether** ?

6. Comet Isikiel was viewed by Julie through her telescope twice.
    The first time was at 2257 on January 8th.
    She next saw it at 0027 on January 10th.
    How much time had passed between her 2 sightings ?

7. a   How many seconds are there in April ?
    b   George is celebrating his 10th birthday. Approximately, how many seconds has he been alive ?

Be able to
read
stopwatches
and time events

For accuracy, especially in sport, time is measured in minutes and seconds, *and the seconds are sometimes measured to 1 or 2 decimal places.*

Revision Example :-

4 mins	30 secs
+ 5 mins $_1$	50 secs
10 mins	20 secs

80 secs = 1 min 20 secs

This stopwatch shows the time in minutes and seconds.

The time shown is
4 minutes 13·07 seconds.

04:13:07

stop watch
PS-50

Exercise 4

1. **Revision**

   a   Round the following times to the **nearest second** :-

   (i)   32·9 secs   (ii)   3 mins 15·3 secs   (iii)   8 mins 7·62 secs.

   b   Change each of these to **minutes** and **seconds** :-

   (i)   84 secs   (ii)   187 secs   (iii)   510 secs.

   c   Change each of these to **hours** and **minutes** :-

   (i)   73 mins   (ii)   145 mins   (iii)   348 mins.

   d   Copy the following and complete :-

(i)	2 mins	40 secs	(ii)	1 hr	55 mins	(iii)	5 mins	20 secs
	+ 3 mins	35 secs		+ 7 hrs	35 mins		− 2 mins	30 secs

2. Round the following times to **1 decimal place** :- (e.g. 4·36 secs —> 4·4 secs)

   a   3·87 secs   b   5·02 secs   c   12·58 secs

   d   18·64 secs   e   24·156 secs   f   7·99 secs

   g   5·443 secs   h   19·777 secs   i   0·351 secs.

3. Here are the times for the first 6 runners to finish a 400 metre race :-

Samson - 45·27 secs	Thomson - 46·36 secs	McGovern - 44·78 secs
Murray - 46·45 secs	Goodwin - 45·08 secs	Van Zanten - 46·09 secs

   List the 6 runners in order, **winner first**.

4. Here are the individual times for each of the four runners for a top USA team in the 4 by 400 metre relay race in an event in Germany.

Morry - 44·61 secs,   Johnstone - 43·28 secs,   Watt - 42·94 secs,   Reynold - 43·78 secs

Calculate the **total** time they took for the race.
   (*Give your answer in minutes and seconds*).

5. Here are the times for the four British runners :-

Steel - 44·59 secs,   Tobine - 43·76 secs,   Breingan - 43·1 secs,   Ronson - 43·69 secs

Calculate the total time the British team took. Which team was faster ?

6. At the Olympic games in Beijing 2008, Shelley-Ann Fraser of Jamaica, ran the women's 100 metre race in 10·78 seconds followed by compatriots Sherone Simpson and Kerron Stewart, both on 10·97 seconds. Lauryn Williams (USA) finished fourth, with a time of 11·03 seconds.

   By how much did Fraser beat Williams ?

7. Tirunesh Dibaba broke her own women's 5000 metre world indoor record of 14 minutes 32·91 seconds at the Boston Indoor Games in 2007 by 5·49 seconds.

   What was her new world record time ?

8. This stopwatch shows the time in minutes and seconds.

   The time shown is **7 minutes 23·95 seconds.**

   State the times which are shown on the
   following stopwatches :-

a   b   c   d   e

9. The tachograph* on a minibus shows how long a driver has been driving. The times are in hours, minutes and seconds.

   Write down these times :-

a  b  c

   *   A tachograph is used to control how long lorry and bus drivers drive without a break.

10.   Lucas won the race in a time of 1 minute 12·3 seconds.

Sidwell was only $\frac{9}{10}$ of a second behind him.

What was Sidwell's time ?

11. Look at the lap times for 2 motocross bikers.

    a   Who was faster, Pete or Cliff ?

    b   How much faster was one than the other ?

12.  Gregor's lap time in the same race was 2 minutes 55·88 seconds.

    a   How much faster was Gregor than Pete ?

    b   The slowest time in the race was by Billy.
He was 4·04 seconds slower than Pete.

        What was Billy's time ?

13. Look at the times for 2 runners in a 1500 metres race.

Mason and Selleck finished well ahead of the other runners.

    a   Who won, Mason or Selleck ?

    b   By how many seconds had the winner
beaten the runner-up ?

    c   Segal was third, 1·25 seconds behind the runner-up.

        What was Segal's time for the race ?

14.  Paula's time for the marathon is shown on this stopwatch.

Amanda's time was 2 hours 46 minutes 30·35 seconds.

    a   By how much had Paula beaten Amanda ?

    b   The last runner in the race crossed the finishing
line 4 hours 10 minutes 42·75 seconds after Paula.

        What was her time ?

15. Helga and Ingrid are training for a marathon.

Helga lives on an island and Ingrid lives on the mainland.

Helga plans to leave from her house and run over
every one of the 7 bridges only once before
ending up at Ingrid's house.

Make a copy of the map.

Can you find a route for Helga ?

Remember to cross every bridge but only once.

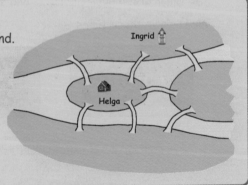

1. 0530 can be written as "half past five in the morning".

Write these times in words :- a `07:52`   b `22:47`

2. Write the time shown on this clock in am/pm notation.

home from school

3. Write the times shown below as 24 hour times :-

   a 8.17 pm   b twenty to five in the morning

   c 11.29 pm   d seven minutes to nine at night.

4. Write these as 12 hour times :-

   a 0245   b 1709   c 2157.

5. Here are the times of two leisure cruises down the west coast of Scotland.

	Ullapool	Mallaig	Fort William	Oban	Greenock	Ayr	Stranraer
Early dep.	0845	1134	1520	1725	1958	2112	2245
Late dep.	1330	1619	2105				

a How long does it take from Mallaig to Oban ?

b How long does the Early sail take ?

c Assuming both sails take the same time, at what time would the Late sail pass Ayr ?

6. A timetable for a special Senior Citizens Minibus is shown.

   a When the Minibus leaves Erskine at 09.10, at what time does it arrive at Wemyss Bay ?

   b The Minibus arrives at Wemyss Bay at 22.25.

   Where did it set out from and when did it leave ?

Erskine		Langbank		Greenock		Wemyss Bay	
Arrive	Depart	Arrive	Depart	Arrive	Depart	Arrive	Depart
	09.10	09.28	09.30	09.54	09.56	10.25	10.27
12.05	12.10	12.28	12.30	12.54	12.56	13.25	13.27
14.05	15.10	15.28	15.30	15.54	15.56	16.25	16.27
16.05	18.10	18.28	----	----	----	----	----
----	----	----	21.30	21.54	21.56	22.25	----

   c I am at the bus stop in Langbank at 6.15 pm.

   How long do I have to wait for the next Wemyss Bay bus to come along ?

   d How long does the journey take from :-

   (i) Erskine to Langbank   (ii) Erskine to Greenock

   (iii) Langbank to Greenock   (iv) Erskine to Wemyss Bay ?

7. Round to the nearest second :-

   a   12·6 secs   b   38·47 secs   c   1 min 17·75 secs   d   56 min 53·5 secs.

8. Change the following into minutes and seconds :-

   a   70 secs   b   132 secs   c   201 secs   d   390 secs.

9. Write these in hours and minutes :-

   a   86 mins   b   150 mins   c   193 mins   d   423 mins.

10. Here are the times taken by four horses to jump six fences :-

    > Masie - 24·68 secs   Dandie - 23·46 secs
    >
    > Lucy - 24·72 secs   Cherrie - 23·4 secs.

    Find the total time they took to jump the fences,
    answering in minutes and seconds.

11. Copy and complete :-

    a   4 mins   25 secs   b   6 hrs   15 mins
        + 5 mins   55 secs   - 2 hrs   40 mins

12.    There are two films showing in the cinema this weekend.

    "Alien Zombies" which lasts for
    1 hour 56 minutes and "Pirates of
    the Amazon" lasting for 2 hours
    35 minutes.
    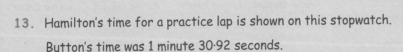
    a   How much shorter is "Alien Zombies" ?

    b   I decide to watch both films, taking a
        half hour break between them.

        How long will that be in total ?

13. Hamilton's time for a practice lap is shown on this stopwatch.

    Button's time was 1 minute 30·92 seconds.

    a   By how much did Button beat Hamilton ?

    b   The fastest practice lap was done by Alonso, and
        was $\frac{3}{100}$ of a second faster than Button.

    What was Alonso's time ?

Consolidation of Decimals

What is a Decimal number ?

Calculators should **NOT** be used in this Chapter unless otherwise instructed

1. In this question, stands for 1 (whole number).

    What do the following diagrams represent ?

    a   b 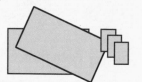   c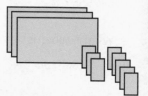

2. A circle has been divided into 10 sections.
    The remaining pink part represent 0·8.

    What decimal number does each of the following represent ?

    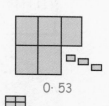

    a   b

    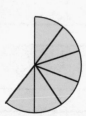   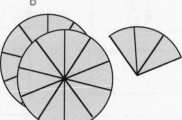

3. The blue diagram shown represents the decimal number 0·53.

    Write down the number represented by each diagram below :–

    0· 53

    a   b 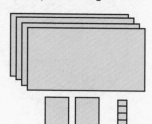   c

4. In the decimal number 14·293, what does the :–   a 9 represent   b 3 represent ?

5. What does the 2 represent in each of the following decimal numbers :–
    a 172·633   b 5·028   c 0·2139   d 203·688   e 1·042 ?

6. Arrange the following groups of decimal numbers in order, smallest first :-

   a 1·97, 1·098, 2·001, 1·8, 2·090, 1·898, 1·008.

   b 0·976, 0·967, 0·908, 0·89, 0·977, 0·807, 1·102.

7. The number 3·458 can be thought of as follows :-

   $$3·458 = 3 \text{ units} + \frac{4}{10} + \frac{5}{100} + \frac{8}{1000} \quad \text{or} \quad 3 \text{ units} + \frac{458}{1000}.$$

   Write the following decimals in the same two ways :-

   a 4·738   b 7·285   c 0·416   d 20·502   e 0·013.

8. What number is :-

   a $\frac{3}{10}$ up from 8·4   b $\frac{5}{10}$ down from 8·62   c $\frac{6}{100}$ up from 0·52

   d $\frac{7}{100}$ up from 2·119   e $\frac{3}{1000}$ up from 3·687   f $\frac{9}{1000}$ down from 7·909 ?

Reading Decimal Scales

9. Say what number each of these arrows is pointing to :-

   a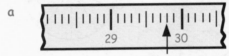
   b

   c
   d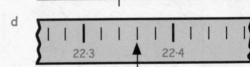

   e
   f

   g   h   i   be careful

   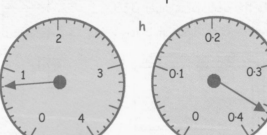
   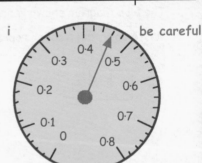

10. Look at the scale below and write down what numbers the arrows A, B, C..... are pointing to :-

    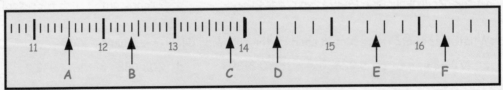

Rounding

11. Round these to the nearest whole £ :-

    a £8·23   b £1·75   c £18·67   d £19·48

    e £11·61   f £0·52   g £0·50   h 18762 pence.

12. Round these measurements to the nearest whole centimetre :-

    a 7·3 cm   b 8·7 cm   c 3·48 cm   d 11·55 cm

    e 13·37 cm   f 69·91 cm   g 41·14 cm   h 99·50 cm.

13. Round these numbers to the nearest whole number :-

    a 1·4 —>   b 4·9 —>   c 8·26 —>   d 36·348 —>

    e 15·74 —>   f 27·059 —>   g 14·755554 —>   h 342·09999 —>

14. Round these numbers to 1 decimal place :-

    a 8·24 —> 8·... b 2·913 —>   c 11·49312 —>   d 18·46576 —>

    e 4·04717 —>   f 14·88437 —>   g 0·34789—>   h 0·08201 —>

15. Use your calculator to do the following divisions, then write down the
    answers correct to 1 decimal place :-

    a 80 ÷ 15   b 5200 ÷ 17   c 17·6 ÷ 0·76

    d 614 ÷ 35·3   e 0·25 ÷ 0·07   f 8000 ÷ 316·9.

16. Use your calculator to change these fractions to decimals and round your
    answers to 1 decimal place :-

    a $\frac{3}{7}$ = (3 ÷ 7) = 0·4285714.... = 0·..... (to 1 decimal place)

    b $\frac{3}{11}$ = (3 ÷ 11) = 0·   c $\frac{7}{9}$ = (7 ÷ ...) =   d $\frac{12}{19}$ =

17. We can estimate answers by rounding to 1 decimal place.

    First, round each number to 1 decimal place, and then find an estimate to :-

    a 4·187 + 7·639   b 17·513 + 38·399   c 11·631 – 5·185

    d 0·665 + 4·714   e 45·966 – 14·515   f 7·287 + 0·176

18. Round these numbers to 2 decimal places :-

    a 9·367 —> 9·3... b 3·854 —>   c 13·26909 —>   d 19·51098 —>

    e 4·00617 —>   f 23·89704 —>   g 0·275—>   h 0·099611 —>

19. a A banner, 7·3 metres long, is cut into 4 pieces of equal length.

       What length will each part of the banner be (to 1 decimal place) ?

    b 11·27 kg of potatoes are placed in equal amounts into 6 pots.

       How many kilograms will there be in each pot (to 1 decimal place) ?

Adding and Subtracting Decimals

20. a 3·8 + 1·1   b 18·6 + 12·3   c 33·9 + 8·4   d 5·73 + 6·5

    e 0·348 + 0·46   f 0·89 + 0·376   g 0·754 + 0·78   h 10·44 + 10·976

    i 25·2 + 15·56   j 19·1 + 2·458   k 703·99 + 84   l 222·7 + 115·658

    m 4·8 – 4·5   n 19·6 – 16·2   o 78·7 – 40·6   p 2·57 – 0·5

    q 47·7 – 34·92   r 718·4 – 511·86   s 3 – 0·084   t 1111 – 100·861.

21. Find the total length or height for each of the following :-

    a

    b

    c

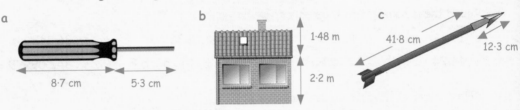

8·7 cm   5·3 cm

1·48 m

2·2 m

41·8 cm   12·3 cm

22. Find :-

    a An empty barrel weighs 8·62 kilograms.
       7·7 kilograms of apples are put into the barrel.

       What is the combined weight ?

    b It is 11·4 kilometres to cycle from my house to the gym.
       Taking a short cut, it is only 8·53 kilometres to the gym.

       How much shorter is it to take the short cut ?

    c Baz collects his paper round money on a Monday.

       He collects £8·75 from Ash Lane, £11·80 from
       Beech Grove and £18·90 from Cedar Street.

       (i)   How much should he collect altogether ?

       (ii) He received £55 including tips. How much did he get in tips ?

    d  Drew cycles 8·7 kilometres of a 12 kilometre journey.

       Tara jogs 4·72 kilometres of an 8·5 kilometre run.

       Who has still to travel the farthest and by how much ?

    e Ally has a square garden of side 8·72 metres.

       Chere has a rectangular garden with length 8·14 m
       and breadth 9·2 m.

       They calculate the perimeters of their gardens.

       Who has the larger perimeter and by how much ?

Multiplying and Dividing involving Decimals

23. Copy the following and complete the calculations :-

    a   23·8   b   142·73   c   345·6   d   974·28

               × 4   × 7   × 3   × 5

24. Rewrite each of these in the above form and complete the calculations :-

    a 7·7 × 8   b 27·5 × 4   c 39·715 × 5   d 6 × 4012·84.

25. Show your working in answering the following questions :-

    aA tray of strawberries weighs 3·2 kilograms.

                  What is the weight of 8 trays ?

    b Henry the plumber earns £38·48 per hour.

        How much does he earn for working one day from 7.30 am till 2.30 pm ?

    c A baby monkey gained 176 grams per week over the past 8 weeks.

        How much is this weight increase in total ?

    d Alex saved £8·85 per week for 6 weeks.
        Senna saved £7·25 per week for 7 weeks.

        Who had saved more money and by how much ?

26. Copy the following and complete the calculations :-

    a $4\overline{)50·76}$ b $5\overline{)79·15}$ c $7\overline{)111·58}$ d $9\overline{)50·76}$

27. Rewrite each of these in the above form and complete the calculation :-

    a 7·6 ÷ 2   b 53·4 ÷ 6   c 12·09 ÷ 3   d 145·35 ÷ 5.

28. Show your working in answering the following questions :-

    a 9 identical stone blocks weigh 433·8 tonnes.

        What is the weight of 1 block ?

    b Sammi is paid £154·64 for working 8 hours as a surveyor.

        How much does she earn each hour ?

    c A distance runner practised the same route each day for 9 days.
        He covered a total distance of 131·67 kilometres.

        What was the distance of the route each day ?

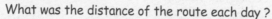

29. Write down the answers to the following :-

    a 8.6×10 b 1.8×10 c 10×1.01 d 10×0.02

    e 32.387×10 f 5.101×10 g 10×0.007 h 0.0102×10.

30. Write down the answers to :-

    a 5.32×100 b 9.44×100 c 100×2.03 d 100×5.5

    e 11.123×100 f 100×0.155 g 100×0.0176 h 0.0094×100.

31. Write down the answers to :-

    a 1.147×1000 b 6.060×1000 c 1.34×1000 d 1000×56.1

    e 1000×0.789 f 0.0654×1000 g 1000×1.0101 h 1000×0.7007.

32. A large jar of jam weighs 4·4 pounds. What is the weight of :-

    a 10 jars   b 100 jars   c 1000 jars ?

33. There are 1000 grams in 1 kilogram. How many grams are there in :-

    a 8·435 kg   b 91·7 kg   c 0·1 kg   d 0·001 kg ?

34. Write down the answers to the following :-

    a $43.1 \div 10$ b $88.8 \div 10$ c $23.05 \div 10$ d $15 \div 10$

    e $9 \div 10$ f $0.54 \div 10$ g $0.6 \div 10$ h $0.011 \div 10$.

35. Do the following :-

    a $159.5 \div 100$ b $753.32 \div 100$ c $45.1 \div 100$ d $87.04 \div 100$

    e $880 \div 100$ f $95 \div 100$ g $1.1 \div 100$ h $0.5 \div 100$.

36. Find :-

    a $3598.2 \div 1000$ b $32\,5876 \div 1000$ c $4560 \div 1000$ d $834.1 \div 1000$

    e $120 \div 1000$ f $400 \div 1000$ g $34.3 \div 1000$ h $11 \div 1000$.

37. a   The total weight of 100 safety pins is 121 grams.

                    What is the weight of 1 safety pin ?

    b   10 people shared a £175·80 bill in a restaurant.

         How much did each person have to pay ?

    c   One thousand people each paid £33·20 into a charity last week.

         How much did the charity receive last week ?

Mixed problems

38. Round each of the following to the number of decimal places shown in each bracket :–

   a   2·641   (1 decimal place)   b   18·951   (1)   c   0·8499   (1)

   d   9·16789   (2)   e   0·07651   (2)   f   99·765   (2).   g   0·00796   (2)

39. Write down the answers to the following :–

   a   8·8 + 1·11   b   12·6 – 8·9   c   33·9 x 4   d   5·75 ÷ 5

   e   0·348 x 100   f   0·89 ÷ 10   g   1000 x 2·583   h   10 x 1·976

   i   25·2 x 7   j   19·1 x 100   k   703·98 ÷ 3   l   111·7 + 11·527

   m   403·8 – 47·52   n   16 ÷ 100   o   0·004 x 10   p   100 x 0·1 x 10.

40. a   A joiner has a 4·65 metre plank of wood.

   They cut off a 2·8 m and a 0·82 m piece.

   How much of the plank is remaining ?

   b    Jane has a bookshelf. She can fill the bookshelf
   by stacking 4 books which are 6·74 cm wide.

   Find the length of the shelf.

   c   Farmer Todd has a field which is 112·5 metres wide.
   He creates 9 equally spaced rows in the field to plant beetroot.

   Calculate the width of each row.

   d   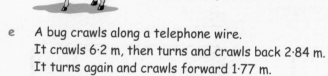 A gardener buys 124·8 kilograms of horse manure for his field.
   The manure is spread into equal amounts over 8 areas of his garden.

   How much is spread over each area ?

   e   A bug crawls along a telephone wire.
   It crawls 6·2 m, then turns and crawls back 2·84 m.
   It turns again and crawls forward 1·77 m.

   How far is the bug from its starting point ?

41. Calculate. (*Hint* – use BOMDAS).

   a   4 + 5 x 2   b   11 – 3 x 3   c   3 x 4 – 8 ÷ 2

   d   10 + 8 ÷ 4 – 6   e   20 – 16 ÷ 4   f   60 – 50 ÷ 10

   g   20 – 12 + 2 – 10   h   a quarter of 20 ÷ 5   i   a fifth of 50 – 10

   j $\frac{1}{2}$ of 16 ÷ 4   k   10 + $\frac{1}{3}$ of 15   l   13 – $\frac{1}{4}$ of 12 + 2

   m   18 ÷ (6 – 3)   n   16 ÷ (10 – 2)   o   5 x (6 + 3).

Chapter 4

Decimals

Multiplication of Decimals by multiples of 10, 100, 1000

Be able to multiply any decimal number by a multiple of 10, 100 or 1000

Remember :-

> If you multiply by 10,   move all the figures **ONE** place **LEFT**
> *(or move the point one place right).*
>
> If you multiply by 100,   move all the figures **TWO** places **LEFT**
> *(or move the point two places right).*
>
> If you multiply by 1000, move all the figures **THREE** place **LEFT**
> *(or move the point three places right).*

Learn the following rules :-

> To multiply by 20   =>   multiply by 10 then times by 2.
>
> To multiply by 300   =>   multiply by 100 then times by 3.
>
> To multiply by 4000   =>   multiply by 1000 then times by 4.

Exercise 1

1. Copy and **complete** each sentence :-

    a   To multiply by 60   you would multiply by 10 then times by ....

    b   To multiply by 800   you would multiply by ..... then times by ....

    c   To multiply by 9000   you would multiply by ....

    d   To multiply by 70   ....

2. Copy and complete using the rules above :-

    a . 1·32 x 20 =   b   12·213 x 300

    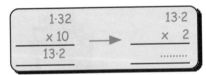   

    c   1·1234 x 2000   d   1·631 x 400

    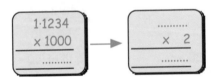   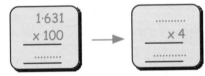

3. Find :-   a   13·23 x 40   b   14·12 x 60   c   3·951 x 90

    d   437·6 x 50   e   23·13 x 200   f   245·3 x 700   g   1·048 x 900

    h   0·076 x 800   i   0·073 x 2000   j   10·97 x 5000   k   0·0078 x 9000

Division of Decimals by multiples of 10, 100, 1000

Remember :-

If you divide by 10,   move all the figures ONE place RIGHT
                        (or move the point one place left).

If you divide by 100,   move all the figures TWO places RIGHT
                        (or move the point two places left).

If you divide by 1000, move all the figures THREE place RIGHT
                        (or move the point three places left)

Learn the following rules :-

To divide by 20   =>   divide by 10 then divide by 2.

To divide by 300   =>   divide by 100 then divide by 3.

To divide by 4000   =>   divide by 1000 then divide by 4.

Exercise 2

1. Copy and complete each sentence :-

    a   To divide by 90   you would divide by 10 then divide by ....

    b   To divide by 700   you would divide by ..... then ....

    c   To divide by 5000   ....

2. Copy and complete using the rules above :-

    a   84·6 ÷ 20 =   b   123·6 ÷ 300

3. Find :-

    a   32·2 ÷ 20   b   137·8 ÷ 40   c   51·95 ÷ 50   d   437·6 ÷ 40

    e   11·46 ÷ 600   f   245·35 ÷ 700   g   9·018 ÷ 90   h   13 ÷ 500

    i   88·4 ÷ 2000   j   96 ÷ 4000   k   0·8 ÷ 5000   l   568 ÷ 4000.

4. Find :-

    a   612 ÷ 900   b   6·07 x 80   c   51·92 ÷ 80   d   436 ÷ 4000

    e   1·29 ÷ 50   f   240 x 70   g   11·4 ÷ 300   h   96 ÷ 6000

    i   17·7 x 70   j   0·99 ÷ 300   k   0·8 ÷ 40   l   0·055 x 9000.

5. Use a calculator to check all your answers.

1. Write these numbers using digits :-

   a one hundred and four

   b two thousand, six hundred and one.

2. Write these numbers in words :-

   a 3402   b 18 006   c 132 500   d 2 675 020.

3. What does the 7 stand for in the number :-

   a 34 171   b 170 020   c 0·8179   d 5·71332 ?

4. Write the number that comes just :-

   a before 1980   b after 120 999   c before 200 000.

5. Rewrite each set of numbers in order. Start with the smallest :-

   a 22 333, 9999, 7654, 19 999, 20 112, 22 121

   b 10·01, 10·99, 10·009, 10·099, 10·0955, 10·19999.

6. To what numbers do the arrows point ?

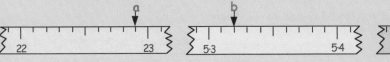

7. a Round to the nearest whole number :-   (i) 31·5103   (ii) 9·4989.

    b Round to one decimal place :-   (i) 5·86   (ii) 53·749.

    c Round to two decimal places :-   (i) 11·1333   (ii) 0·9953.

8. Find :-   a 5·7 + 4·6   b 13·2 − 5·71   c 15·7 × 3

   d 13·74 ÷ 6   e 2·483 × 100   f 117·6 ÷ 10   g 125 ÷ 1000

   h 16·88 ÷ 20   i 1·2145 × 300   j 8·08 ÷ 40   k 0·32 × 2000

9. Find :-   a 3 + 5 × 2   b 25 − 10 ÷ 5   c 20 + 6 ÷ 2 − 13

   d 5 × (6 − 2)   e 18 − 15 ÷ 3 + 2   f 3 + $\frac{1}{2}$ of (10 − 4).

You may use a calculator for Q 10.

10. a Cut a plank 15·24 metres long into 6 equal sections. What length is each section ?

    b A 9000 ml carton of juice holds 12 packets. How many ml is in each packet ?

    c A plumber has twenty four 3·4 metre lengths of pipe. What is the total length of pipe ?

    d There are twenty sweets in a packet. Fifty packets are in a box. 144 boxes in a crate.

       How many sweets are in a crate ?

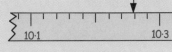

Consolidation of Angles

1. Acute, Right, Obtuse, Straight **or** Reflex. What kind of angles are these ?

   a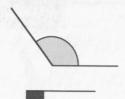

   b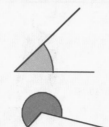

   c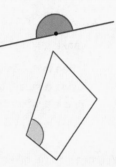

   d

   e

   f

2. From the angles listed below, list which ones are :-

   a acute   b obtuse   c right   d straight   e reflex.

   127°, 53°, 184°, 90°, 300°, 2°, 178°, 97°, 180°, 39°, 126°, 63°.

3. Use 3 letters to name each coloured angle :-

   a

   b

   c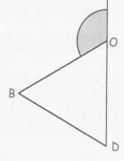

4. Estimate the size of both angles, then use a protractor to measure them accurately.

   a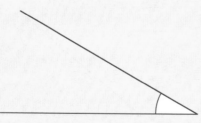

   b

5. Draw each of the following angles and label them with their letters :-

   a   ∠ABC = 30°   b   ∠PQR = 85°   c   ∠XYZ = 150°.

6. How many degrees are there from :-

   a   East to South (clockwise)   b   North East to South (clockwise)

   c   South West to North (anti-clockwise)   d   South to South West (anti-clockwise) ?

Chapter 5

Constructing Triangles

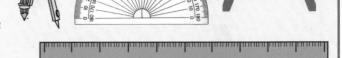

Make an accurate drawing of a triangle, given 2 sides and included angle

The best way to draw a triangle :-

- Make a rough sketch first.

- Then make an accurate drawing using a ruler, a pair of compasses and a protractor.

cm

You need to be given 3 pieces of information about a triangle before you can begin to draw it.

No.1   Two Sides and the Included Angle
(*the angle between the 2 sides*)

Shown opposite is a rough sketch of ΔPQR.

To draw it accurately :-

Step 1 :-   Draw the line PR = 7 cm.

Step 2 :-   Put your protractor at P and mark an angle of 40°.

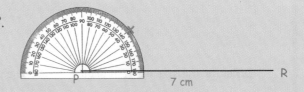

Step 3 :-   Draw a line PQ, from P through the ×, to point Q.

Make sure it is 6 centimetres long.

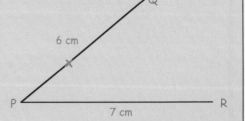

Step 4 :-   Join R to Q to complete the triangle.

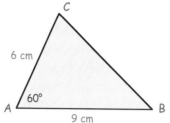

You need a ruler and a protractor for this exercise.

1. On the right is a rough sketch of △ABC.

Follow the instructions to draw it accurately :-

Step 1 :-	Draw the line AB = 9 cm.
Step 2 :-	Put your protractor at AA and mark (with an x) an angle of 60°.
Step 3 :-	Draw a line AC, from A through the x, to point C. (*Make sure it is 6 centimetres long*).
Step 4 :-	Join B to C to complete the triangle.

2.

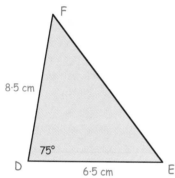

Shown is a sketch of △DEF.

Draw it accurately using the following instructions :-

Step 1 :-	Draw the line DE = 6·5 cm.
Step 2 :-	Put your protractor at D and mark (with an x) an angle of 75°.
Step 3 :-	Draw a line DF, from D through the x, to point F. (*Make sure it is 8·5 centimetres long*).
Step 4 :-	Join F to E to complete the triangle.

3. Make accurate drawings of these triangles :-

a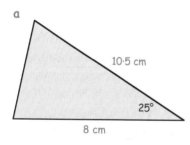

b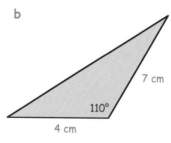

c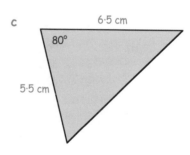

4. Make accurate drawings of the following triangles :-
(*You should make sketches of the triangles first before drawing them*).

a   Draw △ABC where   BC = 6 cm,   BA = 4 cm and ∠ABC = 40°.

b   Draw △DEF where   EF = 8 cm,   DE = 9 cm and ∠DEF = 80°.

c   Draw △GHI where   GH = 70 mm,   GI = 90 mm and ∠HGI = 30°.

d   Draw △JKL where   KL = 12 cm,   KJ = 5·5 cm and ∠JKL = 140°.

e   Draw △RST where   RS = TS = 9 cm and ∠RST = 60°.

No.2 Two Angles and One Side

Here is a sketch of ΔABC,
with 1 side and 2 angles given.

To draw it accurately :-

Step 1 :-   Draw the line AC = 6 cm.

Step 2 :-   Put your protractor at A
and mark an angle of 30°
with an ×.

Step 3 :-   Draw a line from A
through the ×.

Step 4 :-   Put your protractor at C
and mark an angle of 50°
with an new ×.

Step 5 :-   Finally, draw the line from C
through the new × point.

Mark with the letter B, the
point where the 2 lines meet.

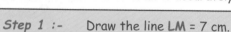

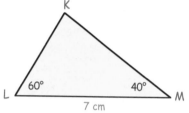

You need a ruler and a protractor for this exercise

1. Shown is a sketch of ΔKLM.

    Follow the instructions to draw it accurately :-

    | Step 1 :- | Draw the line LM = 7 cm. |
    | Step 2:- | Put your protractor at L and mark (with an x) an angle of 60°. |
    | Step 3 :- | Draw a line from L through the x. |
    | Step 4 :- | Put your protractor at M and mark (with a **new x**) an angle of 40°. |
    | Step 5 :- | Draw a line from M through the **new x**, to meet your first line at point K. |

2.

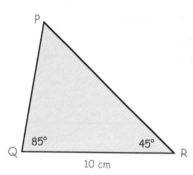

Shown is a sketch of ΔPQR.

Draw it accurately using the following instructions :-

Step 1 :-	Draw the line QR = 10 cm.
Step 2 :-	Put your protractor at Q and mark (with an x) an angle of 85°.
Step 3 :-	Draw a line from Q through that point x.
Step 4 :-	Put your protractor at R and mark (with a **new x**) an angle of 45°.
Step 5 :-	Draw a line from R through the **new x** and mark where the 2 lines cross with a P.

3. Make accurate drawings of the following triangles :-

    a 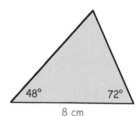   b    c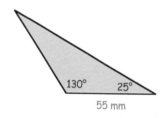

4. Make accurate drawings of the following triangles :-
    (*You should make sketches of the triangles first before drawing them*).

    a   Draw ΔFWR where   FW = 9 cm,   ∠RFW = 50° and ∠RWF = 60°.

    b   Draw ΔTAM where   AM = 11 cm,   ∠TAM = 68° and ∠TMA = 80°.

    c   Draw ΔPON where   PN = 72 mm,   ∠OPN = ∠ONP = 25°.

    d   Draw ΔSME where   SM = 12 cm,   ∠ESM = 28° and ∠EMS = 134°.

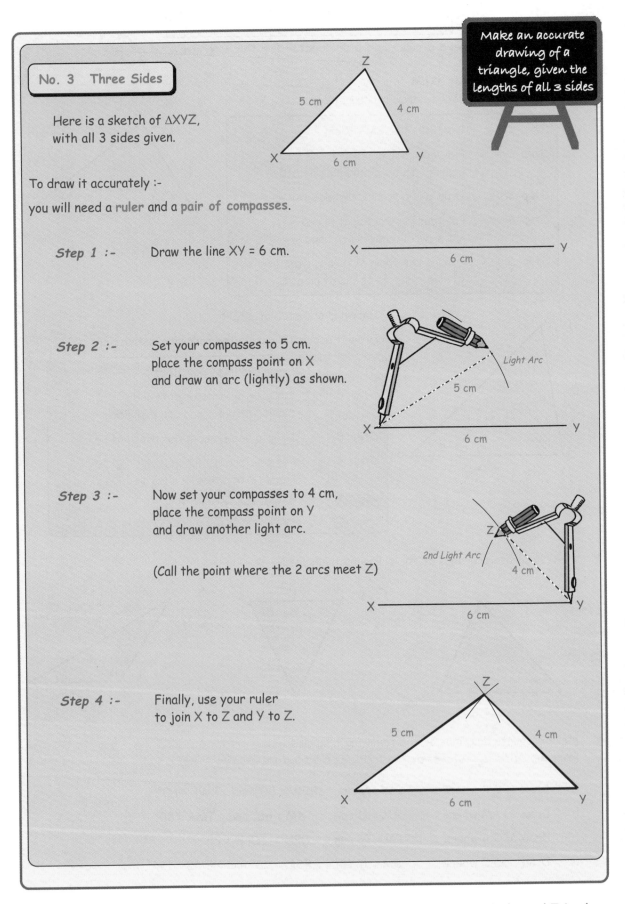

No. 3   Three Sides

Here is a sketch of ΔXYZ,
with all 3 sides given.

To draw it accurately :-

you will need a ruler and a pair of compasses.

Step 1 :-   Draw the line XY = 6 cm.

Step 2 :-   Set your compasses to 5 cm.
place the compass point on X
and draw an arc (lightly) as shown.

Step 3 :-   Now set your compasses to 4 cm,
place the compass point on Y
and draw another light arc.

(Call the point where the 2 arcs meet Z)

Step 4 :-   Finally, use your ruler
to join X to Z and Y to Z.

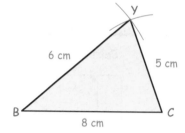

You need a ruler and a pair of compasses for this exercise

1. On the right is a rough sketch of ΔYBC.

Follow the instructions to draw it accurately :-

> **Step 1 :-** Draw the the line BC = 8 cm.
>
> **Step 2 :-** Set your compasses to 6 cm, place the compass point on B and draw a light arc.
>
> **Step 3 :-** Now set your compasses to 5 cm, place the compass point on C and draw another arc.
>
> **Step 4 :-** Name the point where the arcs meet Y. Join Y to B and to C.

2.

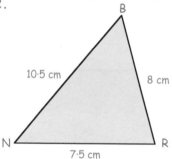

Shown is a sketch of ΔNBR.

Draw it accurately using the following instructions :-

> **Step 1 :-** Draw the line NR = 7·5 cm.
>
> **Step 2 :-** Set your compasses to 10·5 cm. Place the compass point on N and draw a light arc.
>
> **Step 3 :-** Now set your compasses to 8 cm, place the compass point on R and draw another arc.
>
> **Step 4 :-** Call the point where the arcs meet B and join B to N and to R.

3. Make accurate drawings of the following triangles :-

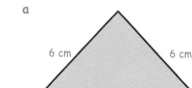

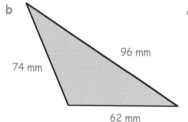

4. Make accurate drawings of the following triangles :-

a Draw ΔCAT where   CA = 7 cm, CT = 5 cm and TA = 3 cm.

b Draw ΔMDR where   MD = 13 cm, MR = 7 cm and DR = 6 cm.

c Draw ΔVKL where   VK = 9·5 cm, VL = KL = 6·5 cm. (What kind of triangle is this ?)

d Draw ΔSPU where   SP = SU = PU = 68 mm. (What kind of triangle is this ?)

5. Try to draw triangle WGR with WG = 8 cm, GR = 4 cm and WR = 3 cm.

Can it be done ? If not, why not ?

Be able to calculate a missing angle

Remember

A right angle has 90°.

A straight angle has 180°.

Examples :- Calculate the value of ? in each of the following :-

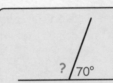

? + 30 = 90

so ? = 60°

? + 70 = 180

so ? = 110°

Exercise 4

1. Calculate the missing value in each of the following :-

a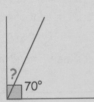
70°

b
75°

c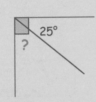
25°
?

d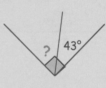
? 43°

e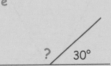
? 30°

f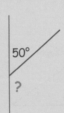
50°
?

g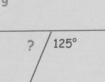
? 125°

h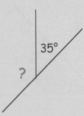
35°
?

2. Calculate the missing value in each of the following :-
(Remember there are 360° round a point).

a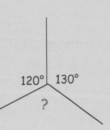
120° 130°
?

b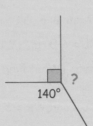
140° ?

c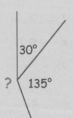
30°
? 135°

d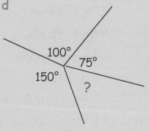
100° 75°
150°
?

The 3
Я's

Revisit - Review - Revise

1. What **type** of angles are coloured ? Answer :- acute, obtuse, right, straight or reflex.

a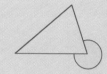

b

c

d

e

f

2. From the diagram, you can see that
   5 is a right angle, but so is (7 + 8).

   Make a list of all the angles from 1 to 11
   that are :-

   a   acute angles

   b   right angles

   c   obtuse angles

   d   reflex angles.

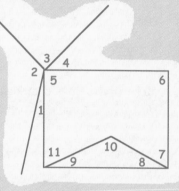

3.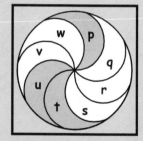

   Write down the new position of the letter :-

   a   **p** when the shape is given a half turn.

   b   **s** under a quarter turn clockwise.

   c   **v** under a quarter turn anti-clockwise.

   d   **w** when the shape is rotated a full revolution.

4. a   Draw any four sided shape which has 2 **acute** angles.

   b   Draw any four sided shape which has 1 **acute** angle.

   c   Draw any four sided shape which has 3 **acute** angles.

5. Name the 2 **types** of angles (one **clockwise** one **anti-clockwise**)
   between the hour hand and the minute hand when the time is :-

   a   two o'clock

   b   five o'clock

   c   1800

   d   2010.

You need a ruler, a protractor and a pair of compasses

6. Use a protractor to measure each of these angles, then write down its **name** and its **size**.

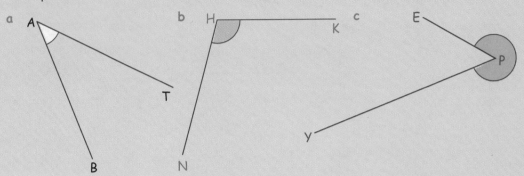

a A ... B ... T

b H ... K ... N

c E ... P ... y

7. Use a ruler and protractor to draw angles of size :-

a   45°   b   170°   c   260°.

8. Make an **accurate** drawing of a triangle ∆PQR
   with PQ = 8 cm, QR = 5 cm and ∠PQR = 50°. (*see the sketch*).

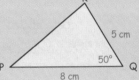

9. Make an **accurate** drawing of a triangle ∆EGH
   with EG = 14 cm, ∠HEG = 20° and ∠EGH = 35°. (*make a sketch first*)

10. Draw a **right angled triangle** with two of its sides 6 cm and 8 cm.

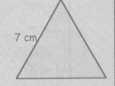

11. Use a ruler and pair of compasses to draw an **equilateral triangle**
    with all three sides 7 centimetres long.

12. a   Use a ruler and a pair of compasses to make
        an accurate, full size drawing of kite VWXY
        as follows :-

    ● Start by drawing line WY = 6 centimetres.

    ● Now draw ∆WVY, then triangle ∆WXY
        using your compasses.

    b   Name the **four** angles of the kite and use a
        protractor to measure and then mark in
        the size of each.

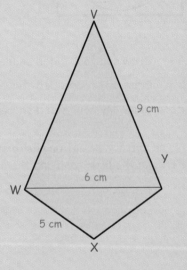

Consolidation of Compass Points

1. Copy and complete the 8 points of the compass diagram shown.

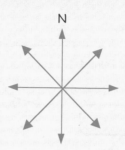

2. How many degrees are there from :-

   a East to South (clockwise)

   b North to South (clockwise)

   c North West to East (anti-clockwise)

   d North to South West (clockwise)

   e N to NW (clockwise)

   f N to SW (anti-clockwise)

3. a  Alice is facing East. She then makes a 45° turn clockwise.

   In which direction is Alice now facing ?

   b Bert was riding his bike North East when he came to a roundabout. He then turned his bike through 45° anti-clockwise.

   In which direction was Bert then travelling ?

   c  A yacht was sailing South West.
   The yacht turned through 90° anti-clockwise.

   In which direction was the yacht now sailing ?

   d A jet is flying SE, away from an airport.

   How many degrees would the jet have to turn to face :-

   (i)   West (clockwise)   (ii)   South (anti-clockwise) ?

4. Use a ruler and protractor to draw an accurate diagram for each of the following :-

   a A bug crawls 5 cm North, then crawls 6 cm West.

   b A slug slithers 4 cm South, then 5 cm South East.

   c A spider crawls 8 cm NE, then 6 cm South, then 4 cm SW.

Chapter 6

Using Scales

Be able to interpret and use a scale on a basic drawing

The map shows Jareed Island.

It has been drawn to a scale of

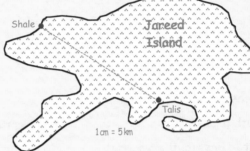

> **1 cm = 5 km.**

This means that every time you measure 1 centimetre on the diagram, in real life it represents 5 kilometres.

If you measure the distance from Shale to Talis on the map, you will find it is 4 centimetres.

=> the real distance between the 2 towns is = **4 x 5 = 20 kilometres**

RULE :-   If you wish to find the REAL distance between 2 places :-

- Measure the distance on the map using a ruler,
- Multiply your measurement by the "scale" value.

Exercise 1

1. This scale drawing of a Gym hall floor is drawn to a scale of :-

   1 cm = 6 m.

   a Measure the length and breadth of the hall.

   b Now calculate the REAL length and breadth of the hall.

2.

   This bus has been drawn using a scale :-

   1 cm = 1·5 m.

   a Measure the height of the bus.

   b Calculate the real height of the bus in metres.

   c Calculate the real length of the bus.

3. This flag is drawn to a scale of :-

   1 cm = 40 cm.

   a Calculate the real height of the flag.

   b Calculate the real width of the flag.

   c Which country does this flag represent ?

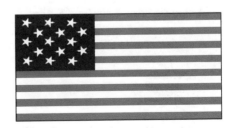

4. A large banner covering the side of a building is to advertise a Rock event.

   The small poster shown has been drawn to a scale of :-

   "Rock Into the Night"

   8th September 2013

   $$1\,cm = 90\,cm.$$

   a By measuring the length of the small poster and using the given scale, calculate the **real** length of the banner (in metres).

   b Calculate the height of the banner.

5. This flag pole has been drawn to a scale of :-

   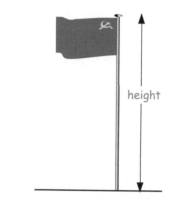

   height

   $$1\,cm = 3\,metres.$$

   a Measure the height of the flagpole.

   b Calculate the **real** height.

6. A rectangular field is used for grazing cows.

   The scale is :- $1\,cm = 40\,metres$.

   a Measure the length and breadth of the field.

   b Calculate the real length and the real breadth of the field.

   c Calculate the **perimeter** of the field.

7.

   This table top has been drawn to a scale :-

   $$1\,cm = 30\,cm.$$

   a Measure the length of the rectangle.

   b Calculate the real length of the table top. *Give your answer in metres (as a decimal).*

   c Calculate the **real** width of the table top.

8. A pipe below has been drawn to a scale of $1\,cm = 12\,metres$.

   a Measure the length of the pipe.

   b Find the **real** length of the pipe.

9. A farmers rectangular field is shown on a map.

The scale of the map is **1 cm = 40 m**.

The length of the field on the map is 8 cm.
The breadth of the field is three quarters
of the length.

   a   Find the **real** length and breadth of
       the field in metres.

   b   Calculate the **perimeter** of the farmer's field.

10. The map opposite shows 4 towns on part
     of the mainland :-

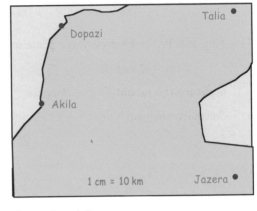

   a   Use your ruler to measure the distance
       from Dopazi to Talia.

   b   Use the scale of the map to determine the
       real distance between the 2 towns.

   c   Measure the shortest distance between the
       following pairs of towns and then use the
       given scale to calculate the real distance
       between them :-

       (i)   Akila and Talia   (ii)   Dopazi and Jazera.

   d   Calculate the shortest *walking* distance between Talia and Jazera.

11.

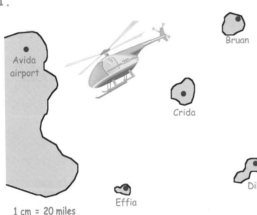

1 cm = 20 miles

A helicopter delivers mail to and around a group
of islands as shown on the map.

The dots show the airports and the landing strips.

   a   Measure the distance from Avida to Bruan.

   b   Use the scale (1 cm = 20 miles) to calculate
       the real distance from Avida to Bruan.

   c   Calculate the **real** distances from Avida to :-

       (i)   Crida   (ii)   Dilum   (iii)   Effia.

   d   The pilot flies from Avida to Bruan, then
       to Crida, Dilum and Effia before returning
       to Avida. How far has he flown altogether ?

12. A cross-country racing circuit
     is shown opposite.

     By measuring the **perimeter**
     of the circuit in centimetres,
     calculate the **real** distance,
     giving your answer in
     kilometres.

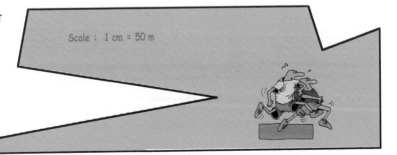

Scale : 1 cm = 50 m

Basic Scale Drawings

Many people use drawings and scale drawings in their jobs.

Without scale drawings there would be no buildings, furniture, cars, clothes, ... the list is endless !

Investigate who uses scale drawings as a large part of their profession.

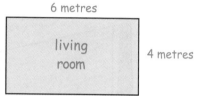

Exercise 2

1. This is a sketch of a rectangular living room.

    Make an accurate scale drawing of the room using a scale of :-

    1 cm = 1 metre.

    6 metres

    living room

    4 metres

2.

    35 metres

    60 metres

    This is a sketch of farmer's field.

    Follow the instructions below on how to make an accurate scale drawing of it using a scale :-

    1 cm = 5 metres.

    a If **5** metres is represented by **1** centimetre in the scale drawing,

    => 60 metres (length) will be represented by (60 ÷ **5**) = 12 cm.

    Begin by drawing a line 12 centimetres long.

    b Next, 35 metres (breadth) will be represented by (35 ÷ **5**) = ... cm.

    Now complete your scale drawing by drawing the width ... centimetres and completing the rectangle.

3. The rectangular door of this garden shed is 160 centimetres by by 60 centimetres.

    Make a scale drawing of the door using a scale :-

    1 cm represents 20 cm.

    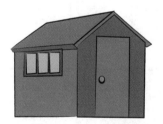

4. A rectangular plot of land 360 metres by 150 metres is used by a company to create a forest for wood production.

    Make a scale drawing of the land using a scale of

    1 cm = 30 m.

5. An orienteering course is designed in the shape of a
    right angled triangle as shown.

    a   Make a neat scale drawing of the triangular
        course using a scale of :-

                1 cm = 200 metres.

    b   Measure the length of the 3rd leg of the course
        on your drawing and use the scale to calculate
        the **real** length of the third leg in metres.

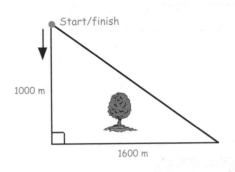

6.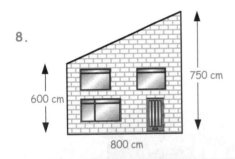

    This triangular flag measures
    150 centimetres by 60 centimetres.

    Make a scale drawing of the flag.

    Scale :-   *1 cm = 10 cm.*

7. A warehouse has a large "L-Shaped"
    floor 23 metres long and 12 metres
    wide (as shown).

    Make a neat scale drawing of the floor
    using a scale of :-   *1 cm = 2 metres.*

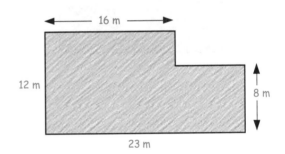

8. This sketch shows the side view of a house.

    a   Make a scale drawing of it using a scale of :-

            1 cm represents 100 cm.

    b   Measure the length of the sloping roof in your
        drawing in centimetres and calculate the **real**
        length of the sloping roof.

9. Shown is the triangular side wall of an Egyptian Pyramid.

    The base of the pyramid
    is 220 metres long and
    the "height" of the triangular
    face is 180 metres.

    a   Make a scale drawing of the pyramid wall
        face using a scale of *1 cm = 20 metres.*

    b   Make 3 identical drawings and use sellotape to construct a 3 dimensional pyramid.

    c   Use your model to find the **real** *vertical* height of this Egyptian pyramid.

Taxing - possibly consider as extension.

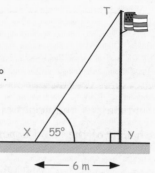

Be able to construct a scale drawing

You will need a **ruler** and **protractor** to draw the figures in this exercise.

Example :-

The sketch shows a flagpole YT supported by a wire.

The distance from X to Y is 6 metres and ∠TXY = 55°.

a Follow the instructions below **carefully** in order to make an accurate scale drawing using a scale of :-

$1\,cm = 2\,metres.$

b Then use your drawing to calculate the **real** height of the flagpole.

a **Step 1** :-   Scale   2 m = 1 cm
       =>   6 m = (6 ÷ 2) = 3 cm.   =>   draw XY = 3 cm.

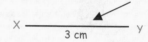

X ———————— Y
       3 cm

Step 2 :-   Draw a (feint) line straight up from Y to show the flagpole

Step 3 :-   Put your protractor on X and mark out an angle of 55°.

X ———————— Y
       3 cm

Step 4 :-   Draw the 55° line from X till it crosses the line drawn up from Y.

top of flagpole

T

b **Step 5** :-   Measure the length from Y to T, where the 2 lines cross (in cm).

Step 6 :-   Multiply this length by the scale (× 2) to obtain the **real** height of the flagpole in metres.

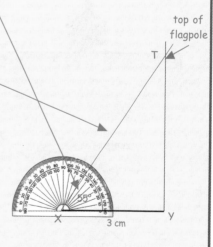

X   Y
   3 cm

The length of the line YT is 4·3 cm. Therefore height of flagpole (4·3 × 2) = **8·6 m**

Exercise 3

1. **a** Make a scale drawing to show the height of this flagpole viewed from point A.

   scale :- **1 cm = 3 metres**.

   - start by drawing the line representing AB.
   - draw a feint line straight up from B.
   - use your protractor to show ∠CAB = 32°.
   - complete the drawing.

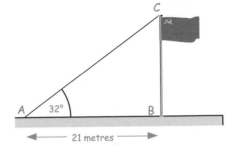

   b Measure, in centimetres, the height of the flagpole in your drawing.

   c Calculate the height of the **real** flagpole.

2.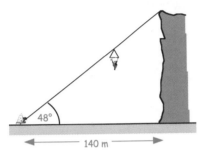

   Ann takes part in a "zip slide" to raise money for charity.

   The wire rope is attached from a cliff-top to a boat waiting in the sea below.

   The angle of elevation of the top of the cliff from the boat is 48°.

   a Make a scale drawing of the boat and the cliff.

   Scale :- **1 cm = 10 metres**.

   b Calculate the **real** height of the cliff.

3. For each of the following :-

   (i) Make a scale drawing using the given scale.

   (ii) Calculate the **real** height of the given object.

a

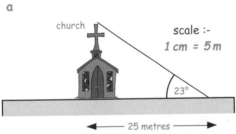

scale :-
1 cm = 5 m

b

scale :-
1 cm = 50 m

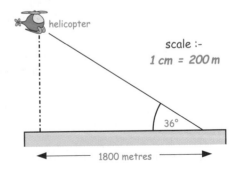

c

scale :-
1 cm = 10 m

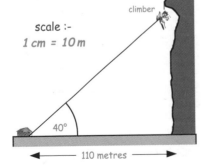

d

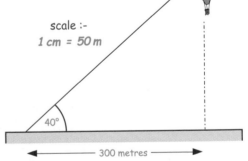

scale :-
1 cm = 200 m

4. The picture shows George Washington, as a boy, chopping down the famous cherry tree.

   a Draw a triangle using the scale

          1 cm = 40 cm.

   b Measure the height of the tree in your figure and calculate the height of the **real** tree.

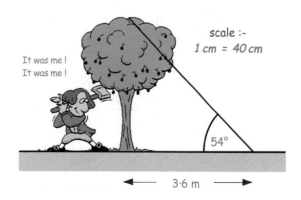

scale :-
1 cm = 40 cm

It was me !
It was me !

54°

3·6 m

5.

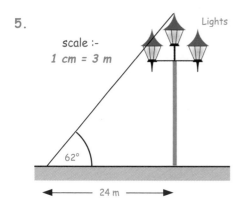

Lights

scale :-
1 cm = 3 m

62°

24 m

Special lights which can be seen for miles are constructed at the end of a pier.

a Make a scale drawing to represent the height of the tallest light using a scale

       1 cm = 3 m.

b Measure the height of the tallest light in your scale drawing and calculate the **real** height of the light.

6. Two soldiers set off from Headquarters (HQ). One of them sets off on a course due West.

   The sketch shows where they are after 4 hours.

   One soldier is exactly North of the other one.

   a Make a scale drawing showing the paths of both soldiers using the scale

          1 cm = 2·5 km.

   b Calculate how far apart the 2 soldiers are at the end of the 4 hours.

   c How many kilometres had Joe travelled ?

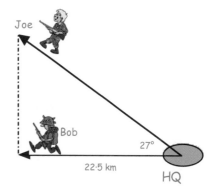

Joe

Bob

27°

22·5 km

HQ

7. The diagram shows the journey made by a small boat as it sailed to two islands.

   The boat travelled from the mainland to Duff Island to Homer Isle then back to the mainland.

   Find the total distance that the boat travelled.

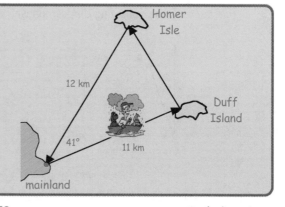

Homer
Isle

12 km

Duff
Island

41°

11 km

mainland

3 Figure Bearings

Another way of describing a direction is to give it as a 3 figure bearing.

A 3-figure bearing must ALWAYS :-

- be measured from the *North*
- be measured in a *clockwise* direction
- have *3* figures.

Examples :- East, as a 3-figure bearing would be
written as 090°. (zero-nine-zero degrees).

West, as a 3-figure bearing would be
written as 270°. (two-seven-zero degrees).

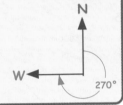

Exercise 4

1. Write each of the following compass directions as a 3 figure bearing :-
   (*Remember your three rules above*).

   a   South

   b   South East

   c   North East

   d   West

   e   East

   f   South West

   g   North West

   h   North.

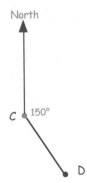

2. Which compass point direction would I be heading
   on if I was travelling on a bearing of :-

   a   135°

   b   270°

   c   315°

   d   000°

   e   one-eight-zero degrees

   f   zero-four-five degrees

   g   two-two-five degrees

   h   zero-nine-zero degrees ?

3. For each of the following directions write down the 3 figure bearing :-

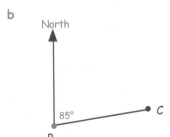

a   North, B, 10°, A

b   North, 85°, B, C

c   North, C, 150°, D

3.

d

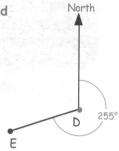

255°

e

187°

f

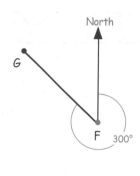

300°

4. (Harder). Write down the 3-figure bearing for each of the following :-

a

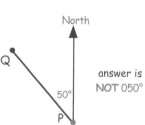

50°

answer is NOT 050°

b

165°

c

8°

5. You should now be able to
    draw an 8 point compass
    N, NE, E, SE, …… etc.

    You should now be able to state
    the 3-figure bearing of each
    of these directions.

    A compass can also be split
    into 16 points (as shown).

    Notice halfway between
    North and North East is

    North North East (or NNE).

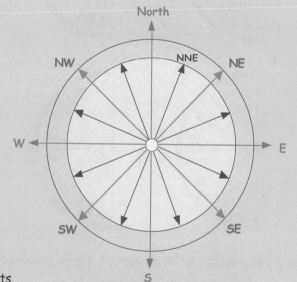

a Investigate the other compass points.

b Draw or sketch this compass rose showing all the missing points.

c Write down the bearings for all 16 compass points.

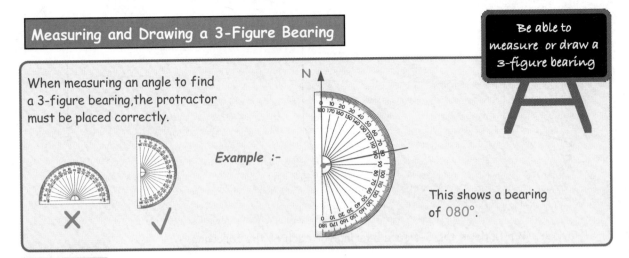

Measuring and Drawing a 3-Figure Bearing

When measuring an angle to find a 3-figure bearing, the protractor must be placed correctly.

✗   ✓

Example :-

This shows a bearing of 080°.

Exercise 5

1. Write down the 3-figure bearing for each of the following :-

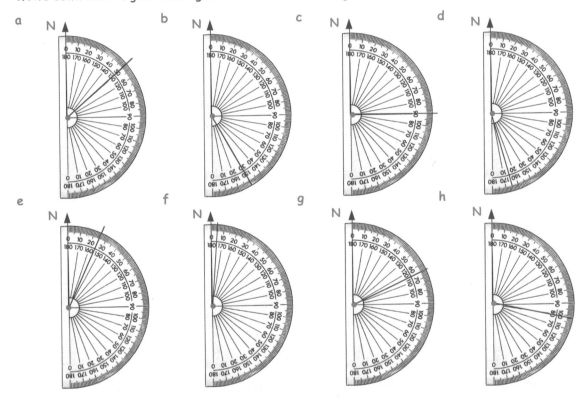

a   b   c   d

e   f   g   h

2. Using a protractor, write down the 3-figure bearing for each of the following :-

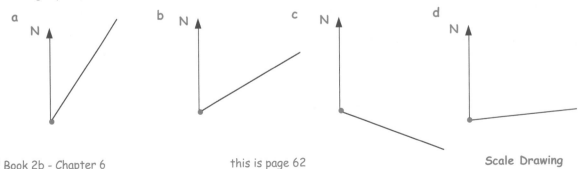

a   b   c   d

2. e  f g h

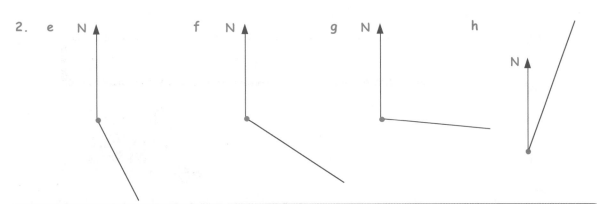

If the direction you are dealing with is further round than south, you still have to measure it "clockwise" from the North.

Can you see that in this figure, the line is 40° further round than south ?

=> it is (40° + 180°) = 220° round from North.

=> the 3-figure bearing shown is 220° .

3. Write down the 3-figure bearing for each of the following :–

a  b  c  d

4. Using a protractor, write down the 3-figure bearing for each of the following :–

a 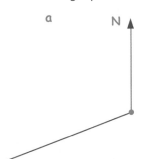 b 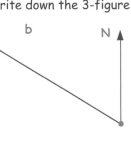 c  d

5. Using a protractor, draw each of the following as a 3-figure bearing :–
   (*Remember to draw a North line first*).

   a 090°   b 140°   c 010°   d 005°

   e 175°   f 200°   g 345°   h 193°.

Revisit - Review - Revise

1. The scale on a map is given as 1 cm = 3 km.
   On this map two petrol stations are 6 cm apart.

   Find the **real** distance between the two stations.

2.  This scale drawing shows a tiled rectangular swimming pool.
   The scale is 1 cm = 3·5 m.

   Calculate the **real** length and breadth of the tiled pool.

3. Make a scale drawing for each sketch below using the scales given :-

   a   1 cm = 2 m   b   1 cm = 25 km.

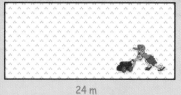
9 m

24 m

100 km

225 km

4. How many degrees clockwise from :-   a   NE and S   b   SW and W ?

5. a   I face NW. I turn 90° anticlockwise. What direction am I now facing ?

   b   I face SE. I turn 225° clockwise. What direction am I now facing ?

6. Measure and write down the bearing of both towns Adford and Byce from CENTRAL :-

   a   North   b   North

   Adford

   Byce

   CENTRAL   CENTRAL

7. a   Make a scale drawing of the diagram
       shown using a scale of 1 cm = 4 m.

   b   Measure the height of the pole on your
       diagram and find its **real** height.

   scale :-
   1 cm = 4 m

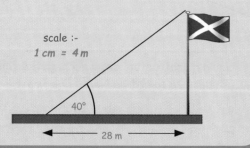
40°

28 m

Consolidation of Money

1. Karen buys a new pair of shoes costing £54·75.

    She hands over three £20 notes.

    a   How much change should Karen get ?

    b   Give an example of what notes and coins she might have in her change.

2. Work out the answers to these :-

    a   £24·63 + £5·97   b   £39·08 - £17·19   c   £5·39 × 6   d   £24·96 ÷ 6.

3. Cookies can be bought in packs of 4 or packs of 6.

    The pack of 4 costs 56p and the pack of 6 costs 78p.

    Which is the better buy ?
    (*Explain your answer with working*).

4.
    "BugKill" spray comes in two bottle sizes.

    * The 500 ml bottle sells for £4·50.

    * The 300 ml bottle sells for £2·82.

    Explain which of the two is the better buy.

You may use a calculator in the next two questions but must show your working.

5. Nine tickets to a premier screening costs £177·75.

    a   What was the cost for each person ?

    b   Mr Paul paid for himself, his wife
        and his friends Julie and Guy Fawkes.

        How much did this cost Mr Paul ?

6. Mrs Talia arranges to take her
    Primary 6 class of 24 pupils to the
    theatre for a Summer Concert.

    a   How much should it cost
        her to buy 1 adult and 24
        childrens' tickets ?

        She then notices the
        "special offer" available.

    b   How much will it cost if she takes up the offer ?

    Summer BandStand
    Adult   £6·50
    Child   £2·80

    Special "Afternoon" Offer

    Buy 6 child tickets - only pay for 5.

Chapter 7

Bank Cards - Debit Cards

Be able to recognise card details from a bank card

Many banks now issue a Bank Card or Debit Card when you open a bank account.

Bank cards can be used in most places to pay for goods or services instead of money.

Memory Chip for Security

PLATINUM SCOTIA BANK

5560 9591 0068 5582

Valid From 04/11   Until End 08/14

MS ANN E STRING   DEBIT CARD

59 82 00   00558260

16 digit Card Number.

Dates are given as month/year eg 08/14 is end of August 2014.

Sortcode identifies which bank branch is being used.

Account Number is the actual bank account number being used.

When using a card you need a secret *Personal Identification Number* (PIN) which ONLY you know.

Exercise 1

1. Look at the bank card above.

   a Which bank has issued this card ?

   b What is the name of the person who uses this card ?

   c Write down the expiry date (end date) in full.

2. Write down all the information shown on each of the following cards :–

   a
   PLATINUM SCOTIA BANK
   2311 3234 5898 0041
   Valid From 02/13   Until End 01/15
   Mrs Ruth Woolie   DEBIT CARD
   20 03 47   00176502

   b
   PLATINUM SCOTIA BANK
   1817 4003 8988 0032
   Valid From 12/12   Until End 11/16
   Mr Alex Dunbeath   DEBIT CARD
   31 45 02   00453198

3. Discuss each of the following :–

   a Why does each bank need a (sort) code ?

   b Why does each person need an account number ?

   c Why should the PIN be secret and known only to the card holder ?

   d Do you think using a card is better than money ?

4. Write a few sentences about each point in question 3.

5. Find out more about banks and banking terms such as ATM, overdraft, direct debit etc.....

Credit Cards

Be able to understand the uses of a credit card

Credit Cards are used in a very similar way to a bank card.

The main difference is that a credit card does not have money stored in an account.

When you use a credit card you are borrowing money (very much like a loan).

Scotia Banks's *Electrik Viza* card has an **APR** charge (Annual Percentage Rate) of 36%.

This means every month there will be a (36% ÷ 12) = 3% interest charge.

Example :- Ms String uses £200 from her credit card.

How much interest will she owe after one month ?

> 3% of £200 = 3 ÷ 100 x 200 = £6
>
> Ms String will owe £206 after one month.

Exercise 2

1. Ms String uses her card (see above) and pays for a new bicycle costing £160.

   How much will she owe after one month ?
   (Remember to use an APR of 36%).

   Copy and complete :-

   > 36% APR means one month is ...%
   >
   > ...% of £160 = ... ÷ 100 x 160 = ...
   >
   > She owes £ ...... after 1 month.

2. How much would she owe after one month if she used £480 on her card ?

3. Mrs Wilson has a *Viza Card* which has an **APR** of 24%.

   a   What is the APR for 1 month ?

   b   How much would she owe after one month if she had
       used each of the following amounts on her card :-

   (i) £780   (ii) £1800   (iii) £345·50 ?

4. Erin uses a *SIMLA* card offering a 30% **APR**.

   How much would she owe after one month if she had used :-

   a   £80   b   £880   c   £2140 ?

5.

Card	APR
Zamex	40%
Vira	33%
Banco	35%

   Paul considers 3 different credit cards as shown.

   Which credit card should he choose ?
   (*Explain why*).

6. a   Find the differences between a bank card, a credit card and a store card.

   b   Many people fall into a lot of debt by using cards. Discuss.

Budgeting

Be able to solve problems involving budgeting

Most people have to budget their money so that they can decide whether or not they can afford to buy certain items.

Example :– Pete saves £35 a week so that he can buy a scooter which costs £840.

   a   Can he afford the scooter after 18 weeks ?

   b   How many more weeks will he need to save ?

> Answer :–   a   35 × 18 = £630.
>   No, he cannot afford it after 18 weeks.
>
>   b   840 ÷ 35 = 24 weeks. He needs to save 6 more weeks.

Exercise 3

1.   Ross is saving £30 a week to buy a ring costing £595 for his girlfriend.

   a   Can he afford to buy the ring after 19 weeks ?

   b   For how many more weeks will he need to save ?

2.    Josh saves £12·00 every week for 9 weeks to buy a pair of hiking boots costing £129.

   For how many more weeks will he need to save ?

3.   Anne saves £25 a week saving for an outfit costing £196.
     Tommy saves £40 per week for a new £275 suit.

   a   Who will be able to buy their item first ?

   b   By how many weeks ?

4.    George saves £25 every week, saving up for a new computer costing £315.

   a   How many weeks will he need to save to be able to afford the computer.

   b   After 8 weeks he notices a sale where the computer is only £225.

       For how many more weeks will he have to save ?

5.   Barry works 5 days a week and has budgeted £60 per week from his pay.

     £40 is for his train fares to and from work and he wants to spend £5 a day on his lunch.

   a   What is wrong with his calculations ?

   b   What should he do to correct this ?

Profit and Loss

Be able to calculate a basic profit or loss

Examples :– If you buy a mobile for £240 and sell it for £140, you have "made a **Loss** of £100".

If you buy a watch for £70 and sell it for £90, you have "made a **Profit** of £20".

> Profit = selling price – buying price, (*if selling price is bigger*).
>
> Loss = buying price – selling price, (*if buying price is bigger*).

Exercise 4

1. I bought a signed football top for £250 and sold it on ebay a year later for £160.

   How much of a **loss** did I make ?

2. I bought a pair of football boots for £32·50 and sold them to a friend for £20.

   How much of a **loss** did I make ?

3.    Barry the builder built a bungalow for £142 550. He sold it for £164 850.

   How much of a **profit** did Barry make ?

4. Ash bought a sculpture for £11 000.
   He sold it to a private collector for £17 500.

   How much of a profit did he make ?

5. Claire bought a pair of shoes for £120 and a designer bag for £195.
   One year later she sold the shoes for £75 and the bag for £256.

   Did she make a profit or loss and by how much ?

6.   Sari bought two paintings for a **total** of £1050. She sold one for £830 and the other for £650.

   How much profit did Sari make altogether ?

7. Eva bought a second hand car for £7150.
   When Eva sold it a year later, she made a loss of £1750.

   For how much did Eva sell the car ?

8.    I bought some film memorabilia for £1375. I sold it 3 years later at a profit of £1120.

   How much did I receive for the memorabilia ?

9. Alan bought ten pairs of shoes for £177.

   He sold each pair for £29·50.

   How much profit did Alan make altogether ?

10. A shopkeeper bought a box of 10 large glasses for a total of £32·50.
    He sold each glass for £4·50.

    How much profit did he make altogether after selling all 10 glasses ?

11.  A shopkeeper buys 8 ornamental vases for a total of £260.
    Unfortunately one vase is broken in the shop.
    He sells the seven remaining vases for £46 each.

    How much profit does the shop make from the vases ?

12. A shop bought 50 sets of candy canes in November for a total cost of £70.
    They sold 30 of them before Christmas at £2·50 each.
    The other 20 were sold after Christmas at 60p each.

    a   How much money was collected when all 50 were sold ?

    b   How much profit did the shop make ?

13.  I bought a box of 10 cupcakes for my shop
    at a total cost of £6·20.
    After selling all the cupcakes, I found I had
    only made a profit of £2·30 altogether.

    What must I have charged for each cupcake ?

14. A newsagent bought a box of 200 pencils for £6·50.
    He tied them into bundles of 10 and sold each bundle for 60p.

    a   How many bundles of 10 pencils did he make ?

    b   How much money did he make when he sold all the pencils ?

    c   How much profit did he make altogether ?

15. Alexandria bought 300 blank DVD's for £150.
    She packed them in envelopes holding 20 discs each and
    sold each pack for £11·50.

    a   How many packs of 20 DVD's did she sell ?

    b   How much money did she make when she sold all the packs ?

    c   How much profit did she make altogether ?

16. Ed pays £60 for 18 identical teddy bears for his shop.

    If he wants to make a profit of £30, how much
    does he need to sell each teddy for ?

Discount

DISCOUNT means **money taken off** the original value of an item.

Be able to understand and calculate a discount

Examples :-

a   A discount of £8 is given on a £26 book.

How much will the book now cost ?

Old price	£26
Discount	£8
New price	£26 – £8 = £18

b   A toy costing £30 has a 10% discount. How much will the toy now cost ?

Old price		£30
Discount (10%)	= $\frac{1}{10}$ of £30 =	£3
New price	= £30 – £3 =	£27

Exercise 5

1.   Find the cost of each item **after** the discount :-

   a   Cost £72

   Discount £17

   b   Cost £175

   Discount £55

   c   Cost £265

   Discount £110

   d   Cost £2400

   Discount 25%

   e   Cost £280

   Discount 50%

   f   Cost £7·50

   Discount 10% .

2.   a   Amy joins a Gym class which usually costs £175.

   She is given an *introductory* discount of £52.

   How much does Amy pay ?

   b   Alice bought a £225 exercise bike but was given a £70 discount.

   How much did Alice pay for her exercise bike ?

   c   Alan bought a barbecue for £160. He was given a 10% discount.

   How much did he pay for his BBQ ?

   d   Pierre bought a chef's outfit costing £76 and got a 25% discount.

   How much did he pay for his outfit ?

3.   a   Sally bought a dress and paid £45, which included a discount of £12.

   How much was the dress originally (before the discount) ?

   b   Sally also bought a pair of shoes which had a 10% discount.

   If she saved £15 in the sale, how much were the shoes before the discount ?

Hire Purchase

Imagine you wanted to buy a washing machine, but you did not have the cash to purchase it.

You can do a deal with the shop, whereby you leave a small **deposit** (say £40) and agree to pay up the **balance** each month over a year.

This is called a "Hire Purchase" (or HP) agreement.

Diamonte
£310

To work out how much you pay for the washing machine using hire purchase (H.P.)

* Do you notice that this has worked out £30 dearer (£340 – £310).

Deposit –	=	£40
+ 12 payments x £25	=	£300
Total Cost	=	£340

This is the DOWN-SIDE of Hire Purchase – it costs you more !!

Discuss why many people use **HP** as a form of paying for goods.

Exercise 6 (Show all your working and set each question down as shown above).

1. A cooker costs £750 cash.
   I can buy it using a Hire Purchase agreement by making

   – a deposit of £50
   – plus 12 monthly payments of £65.

   a Copy this working and complete it.

Deposit –		£ 50
+ 12 payments x £65	=	£ ?
Total H.P. price	=	£ ?

Cash Price £750

H.P. – Deposit £50
   + 12 payments of £65

   b How much did it cost altogether using Hire Purchase ?

   c How much would I have saved by paying cash ?

2.
   Alan's Amazing Autos

   Cash Price – £1800

   Ian bought a second hand car using Hire Purchase. He paid a deposit of £250 and agreed to make **18** monthly payments of £105 each.

   a Copy the working and complete it.

Deposit –		£ ?
+ 18 payments x £105 =		£ ?
Total H.P. price =		£ ?

   b How much **extra** had Ian paid for the car ?

3. Jill bought a new computer from "CompuShop".

   She paid a deposit of £75 and followed this with
   9 monthly payments of £110·50.

   Cash price
   £950

   a   Calculate how much Jill paid in total
       using the Hire Purchase method.
       (Show your three lines of working)

   b   How much **cheaper** would it have been if she had paid cash ?

4. The Persian rug for my living room is priced £4650.
   I couldn't afford to pay cash so I took out a Hire
   Purchase agreement.
   The deposit was £400 and the 15 monthly
   payments were £320·20 each.

   a   How much did it cost me for the rug on H.P. ?

   b   How much **more** was this than the cash price ?

5. When Sally and Nick had their first baby they bought
   a new pram from "Pram–Care" priced £295.
   They bought it on Hire Purchase by making a deposit
   of £20 followed by 26 weekly payments of £12·50.

   a   How much did they pay for the pram using H.P. ?

   b   How much **more** was this than the cash price ?

6.

   Cash price £12500

   Farmer Gregson bought a tractor from "Farming Supplies".

   He took out a Hire Purchase agreement paying a deposit of
   £2500 followed by 24 payments of £462·50.

   a   How much did the tractor cost altogether using H.P. ?

   b   How much **more** was this than the cash price ?

7. Emma bought a TV from Electra–Save costing £365.
   She paid a deposit of £50 and made 6 payments of £52·50 each.

   a   Calculate the total cost of the TV using Hire Purchase.

   b   Did it cost her any more using this method than if she had paid cash ?

   c   Why do you think some shops don't charge more when you take out
       a short term hire purchase agreement ?

8. Sometimes a hire purchase agreement doesn't cost you any more money.
   David wanted to buy a new motorbike which was priced at £1500.

   The salesman allowed him to make a deposit of £300 and
   pay the balance over 6 months at **no extra cost**.

   a   After making the £300 deposit, how much did David still owe ?

   b   If he paid this evenly over the 6 months, how much did he pay each month ?

9.  Lucy bought her designer dress for £650.

She agreed to pay a deposit of £80 and pay the balance over 10 months at no extra charge.

a   After paying the deposit, how much did she still have to pay for her dress ?

b   How much did this leave her to pay each month ?

10. Bill bought a BINDIX tumble drier for £345 from "Ed's Electrics".

a   How much of a deposit did he pay ?

b   What was his monthly repayments ?

Ed's Electrics
No deposit !

Pay back in 15 months at <u>NO</u> extra cost

11.  Leo bought an RXT 1000 keyboard from "Keys Music" using their hire purchase agreement.

Keys Music offered the following :-

> Cash Price - £650
>
> HP terms   –   10% deposit
>   + 9 monthly payments of £71·50.

How much would Leo have saved if he had paid cash ?

12. Emma bought a JetSki.

She paid a deposit of 20% of the cash price and 30 monthly payments of £145.

Cash price
£4500

a   Calculate how much this H.P. agreement cost Emma altogether.

b   How much more expensive was this than paying cash ?

13. Three companies offer different rates of HP for a £3000 jeep.

Calculate the total price for each company and state which is the most expensive.

	Deposit	Equal payments
CheapJeep	£400	12 at £265 each
Jeeps-R-Us	10%	18 at £185 each
JeepCo	12·5%	16 at £175 each

14. The cash price of a holiday was £4000.

Karen paid a 20% deposit and 36 equal monthly payments.

She ended up paying 10% more than the cost price.

How much was each payment ?

Foreign Exchange

Up until 1st January, 2002, all the countries in Europe had their own type of money (currency).

The euro was introduced and the other currencies were no longer accepted.

Britain still uses the pound (£) and when you go to Europe on holiday you have to change your British pounds (GBP) into euros (€).

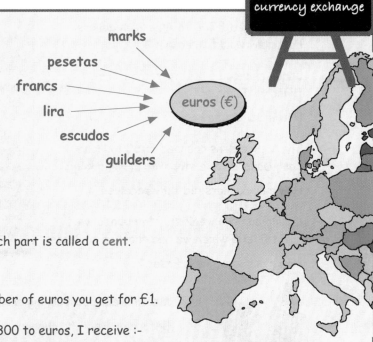

marks
pesetas
francs
lira
escudos
guilders

euros (€)

A euro is divided into 100 parts. Each part is called a cent.

Exchange Rate :-

this is simply the number of euros you get for £1.

Example :- If I change £300 to euros, I receive :-

£		€
1	⟶	1·15
300	= (300 x 1·15) =	345

exchange rate
(as of 1st Oct 2011)
£1 = 1·15 euros

Exercise 7

1. Pauline flew to France and changed £240 to euros. How many euros did she receive ?

2. James changed £500 to euros before going for a week to Rome. How many euros did he get ?

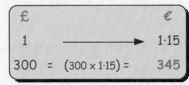

3. Change the following to euros :-

    a   £100   b   £360   c   £820

    d   £2800   e   £25   f   £9·55 (to nearest cent).

4. Find the price of the following when changed to euros :-

    a £23·00

    b £120·00

    c  £13·60

    d £220

    e  £480

    f  £1450

Not every country uses the euro.

Shown are some of the world exchange rates :-

British Pound (October 2011)	
	£1 =
American Dollar ($)	1·70
Australian Dollar	1·60
Chinese Yuan Renminbi	10·5
Danish Krone	8·50
Euro	1·15
Hong Kong Dollar	12·50
Indian Rupee	70
Japanese Yen	120
Mexican Peso	20
New Zealand Dollar	1·90
Norwegian Kroner	9·00
South African Rand	12
Swiss Franc	1·20

5. a If I changed £300 to American dollars how many would I receive ?

    b Jamie changed £800 to Yen before flying to Japan.

       How many did he receive ?

    c The McPhersons changed £150 to Hong Kong Dollars for a stopover in Hong Kong.

       How many dollars did they receive ?

    d During our two week stay in Mexico, we spent £1200 which we had changed to Pesos.

       How much was this in Pesos ?

6.  Martin went backpacking around Australia for 3 months.

    Before he went, he changed £1500 to Australian Dollars.

    How many did Martin receive ?

7. Laura bought a new Samsung Galaxy S11 for £250. How much would this be in :-

    a American Dollars   b Euros

    c Indian Rupees   d Swiss Francs ?

8. I saw the same mobile phone when I was in Australia priced 400 dollars.

    Was this cheaper or dearer than I paid for it back home ? (*Show working*).

9. Decide which is the cheaper :-

    a Scotland - £250,   Germany - 300 euros.

       PS3 Package
       (£250)

    b   Britain - £1600.

       America - $2699.

       imac (£1600)

    c Car price in Britain - £14500.

       Same car in Italy - 16000 euros.

       Only
       £14 500

10. Make up some questions of your own involving currency exchange.

11. Find some currencies that your friends have never heard of and discuss.

Be able to convert a foreign currency back into GBP

In Exercise 7 you learned how to convert GBP, Great Britain Pounds, (£) to Euros (€) by **multiplying**.

If you want to change euros back to pounds => you simply DIVIDE.

Example :- I returned from France with 230 euros and changed it back to pounds. How much did I receive ?

exchange rate
(as of 1st Oct 2011)

£1 = 1·15 euros

€		£
1·15	⟶	1
230	= (230 ÷ 1·15) =	200
	=	£200·00

divide !
divide !
divide !
divide !
divide !
divide !

Exercise 8

1. I returned from Paris with 345 euros.

   If I changed it back to £'s, how much would I get ?

2. Natalie came home from Spain with 92 euros.

   How much did she receive when she took it to the bank and exchanged it for £'s ?

3. Change the following to pounds. (*Give your answers to the nearest penny*).

   a   1700 €   b   315 €   c   1000 €

   d   234 €   e   30 €   f   59·50 €.

4.    When she was in Pisa, Lynsey bought a new dress in one of the fashion houses for 425 euros.

   How much was this in pounds ?

5. What are equivalent values of the following items in pounds (to the nearest penny) ?

   a   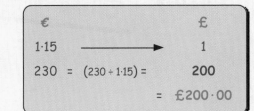   4·60 €   b   11·50 €   c   3·68 €

   d   475 €   e      145 €   f   80 000 €

6. Mr and Mrs Gratton and their two children spend the day at a theme park in Zurich, Switzerland.

Entry to the theme park is :-

> adult - 14·50 francs
> child - 9·50 francs.

How much change (in £) will they get from £50 ?

British Pound (OCT 2011)   £1 =

American Dollar ($)	1·70
Australian Dollar	1·60
Euro	1·15
Hong Kong Dollar	12·50
Indian Rupee	70
Japanese Yen	120
Mexican Peso	20
New Zealand Dollar	1·90
Swiss Franc	1·20

7. Gary bought a MickBurger at home costing £6·80.

It costs $9·90 in America.
It costs $10·40 in Australia.
It costs 299 Rupees in India.
It costs €8·05 in France.
It costs 63·95 Hong Kong Dollars.

In which country is a Mickburger the cheapest ?

8. Alice had £500 to spend on her holiday in Mexico.

She paid 1200 pesos joining a water club and an additional 440 pesos for some water skiing lessons.

How many pounds does she have left to spend ?

9.

Frances is in France buying some presents.

She buys a handbag for 162·50 euros, a bracelet for 66·50 euros and a scarf for 31·00 euros.

She only has £225 worth of traveller's cheques left.

Will this be enough to buy her presents ? (*Explain*).

10. Last year Tommy exchanged £300 for 339 €.

What exchange rate was he given ?

11. How much is $1 worth in Rupees ?
(Hint :- change $ into £ then £ into Rupees).

12. Change each of the following :-

a   100 € to Rupees   b   315 € to Yen

c   180 Pesos to €   d   2340 Swiss Francs to Australian dollars

e $1 million to New Zealand dollars   f   3000 Australian dollars to American dollars.

13. (You will need access to the internet or a conversion table).
Change each of the following and state each country involved :-

a   £100 to Kuna   b   £1000 to SEK

c   £180 to Ruble   d   £120 to Baht.

1. Eddy gave the shopkeeper four £20 notes to pay for his computer case costing £64·75.

   a   How much change will Eddy receive ?

   b   Write down what notes and coins there could be in his change.

2. Find :-

   a   £42·65 + £17·85   b   £173·40 – £12·28   c   £23·66 × 7   d   £155·95 ÷ 5

3. Albert had £136 birthday money.

   He bought a computer game for £42·75, a camera for £39·95 and spent the rest on swimming lessons.

   How much did he spend on swimming lessons ?

4. a      Five girls hire a party bus for £124·60.

   How much should each girl pay ?

   b   Eight boys each pay £8·75 for a football pitch hire.

   How much in total was the pitch hire ?

5. Two boxes of *Super Soap* are shown.

   Which box gives the better deal ? (Explain).

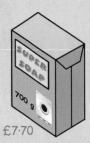

£5·60   £7·70

6. Alex changes £300 into Euros at a rate of £1 = €1·10.

   How many Euros did he receive ?

7. Daria has to choose between two credit cards.
   Emax offers 25% APR and Vista offers 30% APR.

   Which should she choose ? (*Explain*).

8. Jacob saves £14·50 every week for 7 weeks to buy a computer chair costing £170.

   How many **more** weeks will he have to save before he can afford the chair ?

9. Caitlin has saved £85. For her birthday her parents gave her £80, her gran £45 and her brother £20.

   Can she afford to buy a new outfit costing a total of £220 ? (*Explain*).

10. a   Carter bought a new car for £8750. He then sold it for £8900. What was his **profit** ?

    b   Jules sold a case for £86. He bought it for £110. Comment on his **profit** or **loss**.

You may use a calculator for this page.

11. The bank gave Jason a loan. He received all £20 notes and the serial numbers on each note were in numerical order from 144440389 up to 144440413.

    How much was Jason's loan from the bank ?

12. Four Primary schools have collected loose change over the last year. They have 8114 one pence pieces, 975 two pence pieces, 1108 five pence pieces, 609 ten pence pieces and 1380 twenty pence pieces.

    How much money have they collected in total ?

13. Erin changed £450 into Euros at a rate of £1 = €1·15. She spent €375 on her trip to Paris.

    a   How many Euros does she have left ?

    b   If she changed the remaining Euros back into £'s at a rate of £1 = €1·10, how much would she receive ?

14.    George saved £23·50 every week for 24 weeks.

    How many more weeks will he need to save to be able to buy a bike costing £850 ?

15. Mr Thom bought 400 necklaces at £8·72 each. He gave away 50 of them for advertising and sold the rest at £18·25 each.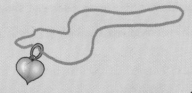

    Calculate his profit.

16. A sweetshop owner buys 30 kg of Mint Imperials for £125·00. He then packs the mints into 100 g bags.

    a   How many bags can be made from the 30 kg ?

    b   If he sells each bag for 80p, how much profit can be made ?

17.    Ella bought a car for £8600.

    A year later she sold it making a loss of 25%.

    How much did she sell the car for ?

18. Petra buys a painting for £1400. A year later she sold the painting and made a 50% profit.

    How much did she sell the painting for ?

Chapter 8

Integers

Be able to work
with integers ...
negative numbers
in particular.

An **integer** is simply a negative or a positive whole number or zero.

Examples :-

   −1, −64, 6, 42, 0, −14, 7 000, −9876, ... are all integers.

   9·5, $\frac{1}{4}$, $7\frac{5}{8}$, −3·9, $1\frac{1}{3}$,   −432·1, ... are **not** integers

Exercise 1

1. A thermometer is the most obvious place to see positive and negative numbers.

    What temperatures are shown here ?

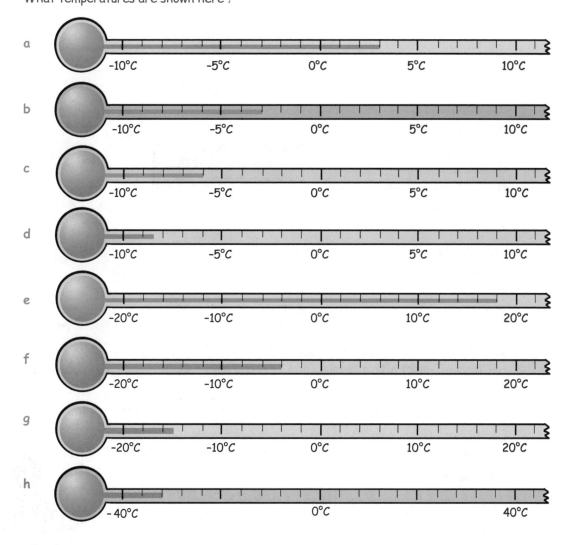

2. Many people *unfortunately* come across negative numbers in their bank accounts.

When you have £200 in your bank account, the computer records this as +£200·00.
You could also be "overdrawn" by £200. This would show up as – £200·00.

a You are **overdrawn** by £50 ! (You **owe** the bank £50).
Write down how you think the computer shows this.

b Write down what these bank balances mean :-

(i)
```
BANK STATEMENT
                    Mr T Jones
                    1 Dye Way
03/01/11            Banff

Balance          + £72·00
```

(ii)
```
BANK STATEMENT
                    Mr B Biggs
                    2 Bray Dr
12/05/11            Croft

Balance          – £55·00
```

On the 3rd of .... I had ..... in my bank account.

(iii)
```
BANK STATEMENT
                    Miss A Bugg
                    4 Harr Ct
19/08/11            Lyss

Balance          £00·00
```

(iv)
```
BANK STATEMENT
                    Ms J Hote
                    The Dorm
30/11/11            Haltord

Balance          – £225·75
```

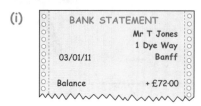

c Sandra's online banking account shows that she has (£50).
She withdraws £55 from the account.
What will her balance show up as now ?

d Jeff's bank balance is shown.
He paid £48 into the account.
What was his new balance then ?

Balance   – £62·00

e Melvin's bank balance was £1. He withdrew £17.
What was his new balance ?

f Last month Lucy's bank balance stood at (–£80·00).
She withdrew a further £25.
What was her balance then ?

g If John's bank balance stands at (–£27), how much would
he have to pay in to clear his overdraft ?

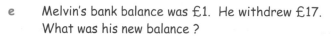

h Moira's online banking account shows that she has (£52·20).
She buys a T-shirt with a cheque for £7·50 and pays £46·50
for messages using her debit card.

When she next logs into her bank's website, what will her statement be showing ?

i Eddie's bank balance on 30/06/2011 was showing up as (–£240).
When his salary was paid in the next day the balance showed (£2010).

How much must Eddie have earned that month ?

j Julie's balance last week was (–£48). She used her debit card for
£60 on the same day as her pay of £300 was paid into her bank.
What was her new balance ?

Negative Numbers & the Thermometer

The thermometer down the side of the page can be a great help when studying negative numbers.

Be able to use a thermometer to help with negative numbers

Exercise 2

1. Make a neat copy of this thermometer in your jotter.

2. Look at your thermometer.

    What is the temperature that is :-

    a   2°C up from 17°C   b   12°C up from 0°C

    c   18°C up from 3°C   d   7°C down from 13°C

    e   12°C down from 22°C   f   3°C up from –1°C

    g   7°C down from –3°C   h   11°C up from –6°C

    i   9°C down from 2°C   j   18°C down from 0°C

    k   12°C down from –7°C   l   16°C down from –5°C

    m   8°C up from –11°C   n   28°C up from –29°C ?

3. 6°C is 14°C up from –8°C.

    Copy and complete these in the same way :-

    (say whether it's .. up from or .. down from each time)

    a   7°C is ....°C up from 1°C   b   12°C is .... from 17°C

    c   0°C is .... from 15°C   d   8°C is .... from –1°C

    e   –9°C is .... from 0°C   f   4°C is .... from –11°C

    g   –21°C is .... from –14°C   h   –3°C is .... from 10°C

    i   40°C is .... from –40°C   j   –62°C is .... from –50°C.

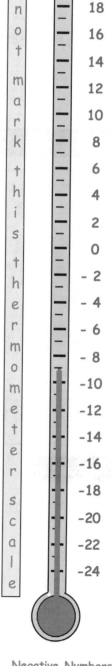

4. One winter's day in Dumfries, the temperature was –8°C.
    In Aviemore it was 7° colder.

    What was the temperature in Aviemore ?

5. As I left my hotel room in Alaska the temperature was 21°C.
    When I stepped outside sixty seconds later, the cold temperature of –23°C hit me immediately !

    What was the difference in temperatures over those sixty seconds ?

6. Whilst on safari in Kenya, I noticed the temperature rose from –6°C at night to 43°C in late morning.

   By how much had the temperature risen ?

7.  Chris made a large batch of chilli con carne and put it in the freezer. Its temperature fell by a steady amount each hour. It started at 9°C and fell to 5°C in one hour.

   What would the temperature be after :–

   a   2 hours   b   3 hours

   c   4 hours   d   10 hours ?

8. Write each set of temperatures in order, coldest first :–

   a   18°C, –2°C, –21°C, 0°C, 1°C, –1°C.

   b   –36°C, –9°C, –17°C, –58°C, 2°C, –2°C.

Adding and Subtracting Negative Numbers

Be able to add and subtract negative numbers

When adding or subtracting negative numbers, draw a thermometer, or at least imagine one !

Example 1 :–   3 + 9

   Imagine the 3 on a thermometer.

   Now do the "+9" by going up 9.   3 + 9 = 12

Example 2 :–   4 + (–9)

   Imagine the 4 on a thermometer.

   Now do the "+(–9)" by going down 9.   4 + (–9) = –5

Example 3 :–   4 – 11

   Imagine the 4 on a thermometer.

   Now do the "–11" by going down 11.   4 – 11 = –7

   15

   10

   5
   (4)

   (–9)   0

   –5

   –10

Exercise 3   Use the thermometer shown to help you with this exercise.

1. Write down each question first, then the answer :–

a	7 + 8	b	4 + 12	c	0 + 14	d	7 + (–5)
e	9 + (–2)	f	13 + (–13)	g	4 + (–7)	h	2 + (–8)
i	0 + (–16)	j	(–3) + 11	k	(–6) + 6	l	(–4) + 21
m	(–9) + 3	n	(–22) + 14	o	6 + (–15)	p	(–4) + (–18)
q	(–9) + (–9)	r	(–5) + (–17)	s	(–18) + 7	t	(–19) + 13.

2. Use your thermometer again to help here :-

(Remember :-   8 – 11 means "go to 8, then move down by 11").

a	12 – 5	b	19 – 19	c	20 – 1	d	5 – 11
e	9 – 14	f	8 – 18	g	0 – 25	h	(–1) – 7
i	(–2) – 5	j	(–18) – 6	k	(–1) – 23	l	0 – 27
m	18 – 38	n	(–14) – 27	o	150 – 450	p	(–159) – 41.

3. The rule is simple.

> • Picture the first number on your thermometer.
> • If you add a positive number move up.
> • If you add a negative number or subtract a number move down.

a	4 + 9	b	6 + (–10)	c	2 – 12	d	(–3) + 13
e	–5 + (–7)	f	14 – 16	g	(–5) – 9	h	(–31) + (–21)
i	–21 + 36	j	0 – 46	k	0 + (–17)	l	(–19) + (–4)
m	17 + (–8)	n	(–16) + 15	o	(–48) + 48	p	63 – 87.

4. Calculate :-

a	4 + (–1) + 2		b	5 + (–6) + 1
c	(–7) + 4 + 5		d	9 + (–8) + (–3)
e	(–12) – 3 – 5		f	1 + (–8) – 7
g	(–3) + (–1) + 8		h	(–5) + (–7) + 11
i	(–6) + (–3) + (–9)		j	23 + (–3) – 21
k	5 + (–25) – 30		l	–100 – 300 – 500

5. Try these :-

a	2 + 3 + 4 + 5		b	6 + 7 + 8 + (–4)
c	3 + 6 + (–5) + (–6)		d	7 + (–2) + (–3) + (–5)
e	(–2) + (–4) + (–6) + (–8)		f	(–3) + (–5) + (–7) + 18
g	20 + (–21) + 9 + (–8)		h	15 – 8 – 3 – 7
i	(–10) – 7 + 12 – 1		j	100 – (50 + 20 + 10)
k	80 + (10 – 20 – 30)		l	–100 – 300 – 500 – 100.

6. a Quickly !! What do you think the answer to 7 – (–1) is ?

If you think the answer is 6 or - 6, you are wrong. The answer in fact is 8 !!

Look at the thermometer, find 7 and -1 and count from -1 up to 7. The answer ??

Find :-	b	4 - (-1)	c	8 - (-3)	d	2 - (-2)
e	1 - (-4)	f	0 - (-3)	g	-2 - (-6)	h	-7 - (-3).

1. State what temperatures are represented on these thermometers :–

    a

    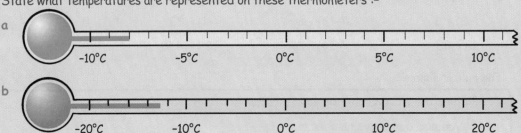

    -10°C   -5°C   0°C   5°C   10°C

    b

    -20°C   -10°C   0°C   10°C   20°C

2. George's bank balance last month was -£350 .

    His monthly wage of £1550 was then paid in, but
    he also paid out his monthly gas bill of £88.

    What is George's new bank balance ?

3.   Pixie had £280 in her bank account before the weekend.

    She withdrew £150 on Friday night and £215 while shopping
    on Saturday afternoon. She deposited £90 on Monday morning.

    Write down her new bank balance.

4. Find :–

    a   6 + (–2)   b   9 + (–9)   c   (–1) + 7   d   (–8) + 11

    e   (–14) + (–13) f   (–3) + (–17)   g   (–26) + 25   h   (–103) – 104

    i   (–5) – 8   j   –15 – 20   k   (–23) + 17   l   (–103) + 104.

5. The temperature at midday on a Spanish beach was 34°C.
    At midnight it had fallen to –6°C.

    By how many degrees had the temperature fallen ?

6.   The coldest temperature ever recorded in Scotland was –27°C.
    (Altnaharra Dec. 1995).
    The warmest recorded was 33°C (Greycrook Aug. 2003).

    Calculate the difference in temperature.

7. Calculate :–

    a   6 – 8 + 1   b   5 – 12 + 2   c   (–1) + 6 – 9   d   (–4) + 9 – 6

    e   0 + (–5) + 5   f   (–6) + (– 1) – 3   g   (–48) + 50 + (–1) h   –50 – 30 – 20.

Chapter 9

Time 2

Distance Calculations

Given Speed & Time, be able to calculate Distance travelled

Imagine you are walking at 4 km per hour and you do so for 3 hours.

Can you see that you will have walked 4 km + 4 km + 4 km = 4 km x 3 = 12 km ?

• To calculate the distance travelled we simply multiply speed x time.

$$D_{istance} = S_{peed} \times T_{ime}$$

Example 1 :-

A car travelled at 45 km per hour for 3 hours.
What distance did it cover ?

D = S x T

= 45 x 3

= 135 km

Example 2 :-

A plane flies at a speed of 180 mph.
How far will it travel in 5 hours ?

D = S x T

= 180 x 5

= 900 miles

Exercise 1

1. Use the rule above (called a formula) to find the distance travelled by :-

   a   Avril, walking at 3 mph for 2 hours
   b   Bert, walking at 4 mph for 3 hours
   c   Carol, driving at 50 mph for 4 hours
   d   Dave, rowing at 1 mph for 6 hours
   e   Francis, cycling at 9 mph for 5 hours
   f   Gerry, hopping at 0·5 mph for 2 hours.

2. Calculate the distance travelled by a :-

   a   lorry, going at 30 mph for 7 hours
   b   train, travelling at 100 mph for 5 hours
   c   plane, doing 380 mph for 4 hours
   d   hot air balloon, floating at 2 mph for 15 hours
   e   coach, moving at 55 mph for 6 hours
   f   fire engine, doing 80 mph for 2 hours.

3. What distances are covered by a :-

   a   speed boat, for 4 hours at 25 km/hr
   b   coach, for 9 hours at 40 km/hr
   c   police car, for 2 hours doing 85 km/hr
   d   person strolling, at 2 km/hr for 3 hours
   e   bird, for 9 hours at 20 km/hr
   f   rocket, doing 2500 km/hr for 20 hours ?

4. A plane left Benidorm at 1325 and arrived in Glasgow at 1625.
   The plane flew at an average speed of 420 mph.

   How long did the flight take and how many miles did the plane cover ?

5. A tug boat left Kincardine at 2.50 pm and sailed at a steady speed of 15 mph along the River Forth.

   How far was the tug boat from Kincardine at 6.50 pm ?

CfE Book 2b - Chapter 9   this is page 87   Time 2

Time Calculations

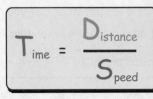

Imagine you travel 12 kilometres, jogging at 6 km per hour.

Since 6 km + 6 km = 12 km, it must have taken you 12 ÷ 6 = **2 hours**.

- If you know your **speed** and the distance you have to travel, you can calculate the **time** taken by dividing distance by **speed**.

$$T_{ime} = \frac{D_{istance}}{S_{peed}}$$

Example 1 :-

A motorbike travelled 150 miles at an average speed of 30 mph.

How long did the journey take ?

$$T = \frac{D}{S}$$
$$= 150 \div 30$$
$$= 5 \text{ hours}$$

Example 2 :-

Glasgow is 540 kilometres from London.

How long will it take me by coach, travelling at an average speed of 90 km/hr ?

$$T = \frac{D}{S}$$
$$= 540 \div 90$$
$$= 6 \text{ hours}$$

Exercise 2

1. Use the formula to calculate the **time** taken for each of these journeys :-

   a walking, 8 km at 2 km/hr
   b running, 24 km at 8 km/hr
   c flying, 2000 km at 500 km/hr
   d driving, 700 miles at 70 mph
   e skating, at 4 km/hr for 12 km
   f crawling, 18 metres at 2 metres per second
   g speeding, at 80 mph for 240 miles
   h eagle, flying at 11 km/hr for 44 km.

2. **When** will these vehicles arrive :-

   a Bus, leaves 9.30 am. Travels 200 miles at an average speed of 50 mph
   b Van, leaves 4.55 pm. Travels 420 miles at an average speed of 60 mph
   c Jet, leaves 2010. Travels 3000 km at an average speed of 500 km/hr ?

3. Goodwin's Removals trucks usually average the speeds shown in the table opposite :-

   For each journey, calculate the time taken.

   > 60 mph on motorway journeys under 130 miles
   > 65 mph on motorway journeys over 130 miles
   > 50 mph on dual carriageways
   > 30 mph on minor roads

   a Glasgow to Stranraer - 50 miles on the dual carriageway.
   b Stirling to Oban - 60 miles on the minor roads.
   c Inverness to Stirling - 120 miles on the motorway.
   d Glasgow to Norwich - 325 miles on the motorway.

This mileage chart shows the distances between several towns.

Can you see that the distance from Tayport to Prestan is 93 miles ?

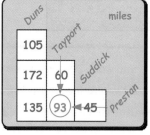

4. Use the chart to find the distance between the following :-

   a   Duns and Prestan   b   Suddick and Duns.

5. Use the mileage chart shown opposite to find the **distance** between these towns and find **how long** each journey should take.

   a   Duns to Tayport at 35 mph.

   b   Tayport to Suddick at 20 mph.

   c   Duns to Suddick at 43 mph.

6. An old steam train picks up passengers and leaves Gretna at 6.45 am.

   It travels the 246 km to Aberdeen at an average speed of 82 km/hr.

   a   How long did the journey take ?

   b   When did the train arrive in Aberdeen ?

7.

A large jet left London's Heathrow Airport at 2130 on a Sunday. Its destination was Mexico, 5580 miles away.

If it travelled at a steady 620 mph :-

   a   How long did the journey take ?

   b   At what time (our time) and on what day did the plane reach Mexico ?

8. Calculate the **time** taken for these long haul flights :-

   a   Paphos - London. Distance 2040 miles. Average speed 408 mph.

   b   Tokyo - Honolulu. Distance 3815 miles. Average speed 545 mph.

   c   Paris - Havana. Distance 7755 km. Average speed 705 km/hr.

   d   Abu Dhabi - Sydney. Distance 12 060 km. Average speed 804 km/hr.

9. List the cities in question 8 and find and write down which countries they are in.

10. A coach driver left Edinburgh at 1000 and drove the 360 miles to Dover to catch the ferry to Belgium.

   · The ferry's departure time was 1730.
   · The coach averaged a speed of 60 mph.
   · He stopped for two half hour breaks.

   Did he make it to Dover on time ? (*Explain*).

11. Calculate the time in hours and minutes for the following journeys :-

   a   Drive the 100 miles from Airth to Bramley at a speed of 40 miles per hour.

   b   Walk for a distance of 21 km at a speed of 6 km per hour.

   c   Cycle at 12 km per hour to Baidmore, a distance of 27 km.

Speed Calculations

Given Distance & Time, be able to calculate Average Speed

Imagine you walk 15 kilometres and it takes you 3 hours.

This means you walked 5 km the first hour, 5 km the 2nd hour

and 5 km the 3rd hour or 15 ÷ 3 = 5 km per hour.

- If you know the distance you have
  travelled and the time taken, you can find
  the speed by dividing distance by time.

$$S_{peed} = \frac{D_{istance}}{T_{ime}}$$

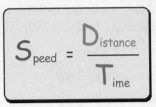

Example 1 :-

A scooter travelled 350 miles, taking a total of 7 hours to complete the journey.

What was the average speed of the scooter ?

$S = \dfrac{D}{T}$

$= 350 \div 7$

$= 50$ mph

Example 2 :-

A centipede covered 12 metres in 2 minutes.

What was the average speed of the insect ?

$S = \dfrac{D}{T}$

$= 12 \div 2$

$= 6$ metres/min

Exercise 3

1. Use the formula to find the average speed of these journeys :-

   a 12 miles in 4 hours

   b 60 miles in 6 hours

   c 240 miles in 8 hours

   d 1000 miles in 20 hours

   e 375 kilometres in 5 hours

   f 560 kilometres in 7 hours.

2. Calculate the average speed of the following journeys - careful with the units !

   a 24 kilometres in 3 hours

   b 320 kilometres in 4 hours

   c 90 metres in 9 seconds

   d 56 miles in 8 seconds

   e 2800 kilometres in 14 hours

   f 2400 metres in 40 minutes.

3. Calculate the average speed of these journeys in miles per hour (mph) :-

   a A train travels 540 miles in 6 hours.

   b A plane flies 1820 miles in 5 hours.

   c A van travels 272 miles in 4 hours.

   d A woman jogs 12 miles in 3 hours.

   e A ship sails 91 miles in 7 hours.

   f A ferry travels 135 miles in 9 hours.

   g A motorbike goes 225 miles in 3 hours.

   h A plane covers 4300 miles in 10 hours.

   i An athlete does 7 miles in 2 hours.

4.   Work out these average speeds :-

   a   A ship travels 48 km in 3 hours.   b   A cyclist covers 64 km in 4 hours.

   c   A runner does 300 metres in 3 minutes.   d   A worm crawls 2 metres in 1 minute.

   e   A girl hops 100 metres in 2 minutes.   f   A fly covers 12 metres in 4 seconds.

   g   A tricycle travels 5 miles in 10 minutes. h   A rocket flies 150 metres in 5 seconds.

5.   A hot air balloon left London at 1130.

     By 1630 it had covered a distance of 65 miles.

     Calculate the average speed of the balloon.

6.

     A plane left Glasgow at 7.45 pm and flew 1107
     miles to Figo in Portugal, arriving at 10.45 pm.

     a   How long did the journey take ?

     b   What was the plane's average speed ?

7.   The first ferry to Liverpool leaves Dublin
     at 0750 and arrives in Liverpool at 1550.

     Find the average speed of the ferry for the 144 mile trip.

8.

     Henry decides to cycle to the coast.

     His outward journey takes him two hours to get there, but the
     return journey takes one hour longer.

     If Henry lives 30 miles from the coast, find his average speed
     for his round trip.

9.   Calculate the average speed for each of these long haul flights :-

   a   Johannesburg - New York. Distance 7968 miles. Time taken 16 hours.

   b   Moscow - Los Angeles. Distance 6084 miles. Time taken 13 hours.

   c   Havana - Rome. Distance 8712 km. Time taken 11 hours.

   d   Toronto - Beijing. Distance 10 584 km. Time taken 14 hours.

10. List the cities in Q9 and state which countries they are in.

11. Calculate the speed for each of these journeys :-

   a   I cycled a distance of 18 km and it took me $1\frac{1}{2}$ hours.

   b   I walked to the shops 3 km from my house. It took me 30 minutes ($\frac{1}{2}$ hour).

   c   The distance from Glasgow to New York is 5200 km. A plane took $6\frac{1}{2}$ hours to fly there.

   d   A lady typed 20 words in 15 seconds. What is her typing speed in words per minute ?

Be able to calculate time, distance or speed knowing the other two values.

It is difficult sometimes to remember which rule to use.

This diagram is called the **time - distance - speed** triangle.

It should help you remember.

- Given Speed and Time   => D = S x T

- Given Distance and Time   => S = $\frac{D}{T}$

- Given Distance and Speed   => T = $\frac{D}{S}$

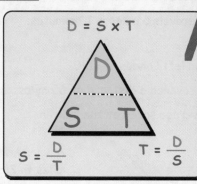

D = S x T

S = $\frac{D}{T}$ T = $\frac{D}{S}$

Example 1 :-

Distance 90 miles. Speed 30 mph.

How long did the journey take ?

T = $\frac{D}{S}$

= 90 ÷ 30

= 3 hours

Example 2 :-

Distance 150 km. Time 5 hrs.

What was the average speed ?

S = $\frac{D}{T}$

= 150 ÷ 5

= 30 km/hr

Example 3 :-

Speed 70 mph. Time 4 hrs.

How far did the vehicle travel ?

D = S x T

= 70 x 4

= 280 miles

Exercise 4

1. Use the correct formula to answer these questions :-

   a   Distance 115 miles. Time 5 hours.   Find the average speed.

   b   Distance 180 km. Speed 45 km/hr.   Find the time taken.

   c   Speed 65 mph. Time 4 hours.   Find the distance travelled.

   d   Time 14 hours. Distance 280 miles.   Find the average speed.

   e   Speed 200 km/hr. Distance 4800 km.   Find the time taken.

   f   Time 7 hours. Speed 308 mph.   Find the distance covered.

   g   Distance 320 km. Speed 40 km/hr.   Find the time taken.

2. A police car chased a stolen van for 2 hours, driving at an average speed of 78·5 km/hr.

   What distance had the police car covered ?

3. A tall ship, sailing at a steady speed, took 3 hours to sail the 54 miles to the island of treasure.

   What was that speed ?

4. This poor chap travelled 144 metres at an average speed of 8 metres per minute after a gust of wind had blown him off his feet.

    For how long was he in the air ?

5. A fighter jet took off from an airfield at 0355 and flew east to meet up with an aircraft carrier at 0755.

    If the jet flew for 2240 kilometres, what was its average speed ?

6.  A cargo ship travelled through 36 miles of shallow water at a slow speed of 4 mph.

    How long did it take the ship to go through this dangerous part of its journey ?

7. A communications satellite orbits a planet at an average speed of 12 800 mph. It takes 5 hours to complete its orbit.

    Calculate the length of the orbit.

8. Postie lives 6 minutes away from the post office depot.
   The distance from his house to the depot is 924 metres.

    a   Work out Postie's average speed, in metres per minute, when he walks to the depot.

    b   If he takes his bike to work he can get there three times quicker.
       How long does his bike journey take ?

9.  A bird flies for 8 days when its migrates from Scotland in winter.

    If it keeps up a steady speed of 235 miles per day what distance will it fly in total ?

10. A snail moves at a very slow speed - sometimes as slow as 5 centimetres per minute.

    At this speed, how long does it take a snail to cross a garden a metre wide ?

11. Walter walked for 3 hours and covered a distance of 9000 metres.

    a   Calculate Walter's speed in metres per hour.

    b   How far will Walter walk in 1 minute ?

12.  It took old Mrs Currie an hour to walk the half mile to the dairy to buy milk and bread.

    Now, with the aid of her new electric chair, she can do it in 12 minutes.

    a   Calculate Mrs Currie's walking speed.

    b   How much faster does she travel in the chair ?

13. a   The 10th February 2001 (10 02 2001) was an 8 digit Palindromic Date.
       (*It reads the same forwards and backwards*).
       Find the next 4 dates after this which were 8 digit palindromes.

    b   2 minutes past 10 on the morning of Jan 10th 2001 (10 02 10 01 2001) was a 12 digit palindrome. Find the next 4 after this.

The 3 Я's

1. Due to extra time and penalties, a football cup-tie which kicked off at 1945 did not finish until 2230.

   How long did the cup-tie last ?

2. a The wedding was to take place at 2.55 pm, but the bride arrived 27 minutes late !

   At what time did she turn up ?

   b The groom had left his home at ten to eleven that morning and had arrived for the ceremony exactly 28 minutes early.

   How long had his journey taken him ?

3. a A cruise liner was meant to dock at twenty five to two on Friday morning, but due to perfect sailing conditions it reached the harbour two hours and thirty five minutes early !

   On which day and at what time did it actually dock ?

   b At 9.30 am a maintenance check, which lasted 8 hours, was then started and carried out.
   After that, the liner set sail on its next voyage, scheduled to last 9 hours 15 minutes.

   When was it due to arrive at its next port of call ?

4.  Singapore is 7 hours ahead of us. When it's 2 pm here, it's 9 pm there.

   The Bennie family flew out to Singapore to visit relatives, leaving London Gatwick at 6.50 pm on Tuesday.

   If the flight to Singapore took 12 hours 45 minutes, on what day and at what time (Singapore time) did they arrive there ?

5. Greenland is 3 hours behind us. I left Edinburgh Airport to explore Greenland at five to four on a Saturday afternoon and arrived there 3 hours and 10 minutes later.

   What time was it when I arrived ?

6. a Given a distance and a journey time, write down the rule (formula) for finding the average speed.

   b Given the average speed and a distance, write down the formula for finding the time for the journey.

   c Given the average speed and the time taken, write down the formula for finding the distance travelled.

7. A van travelled 396 miles in 6 hours.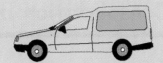

    What was its average speed ?

8.   Mary left her mum's home in Stirling and headed up the A9 dual
    carriageway, driving at a steady speed of 51 km/hr to her own flat
    in Inverness, a distance of 153 km.

    How long did it take her ?

9. A train left Dundee bound for Southampton.
    The journey took 7 hours, averaging a speed of 85 mph.

    How far is it by rail from Dundee to Southampton ?

10. George, a catering manager, drove for 280 miles at an average
    speed of 70 mph to organise a wedding breakfast.

    If he left his kitchen at 3.30 am, when did he arrive at his destination ?

11. At full speed, a tortoise took 6 minutes to cross a garden path, 3 metres wide.

    At what speed did he move, in centimetres per minute ?

12.  Murray can cycle to his friend's in 8 minutes.

    The distance from his house to his friend's is 2400 metres.

    a   Calculate Murray's average speed, in metres per minute.

    If his dad takes him by car, Murray gets there 4 times faster.

    b   How long will it take him by car ?

13. The speed of sound is about 340 metres per second.

    When Harry shouts to Hazel, it takes 3 seconds before she hears him ?

    How far apart must they have been standing ?

14. A spider can cover 80 metres in half an hour.

    Calculate the average speed of the spider in metres per hour.

15. It took a worm 300 minutes, sliding at 7 cm/min to squirm along a patch of ground.

    How far had it travelled, in metres ?

1. Write down the names of each of these two polygons.

2. 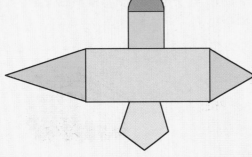   Name all the mathematical shapes you can see in the figure shown opposite.

3. Describe each of these triangles by using an expression from this list.

scalene triangle
isosceles triangle
equilateral triangle

a   b   c

4. Describe each of these triangles by using an expression from this list.

acute angled
obtuse angled
right angled

a   b   c

5. Name and describe these triangles fully.

a   b   c

 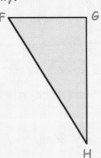 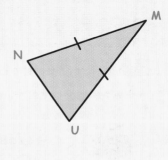

6. 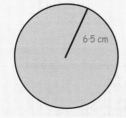   The radius of a circle is 6·5 centimetres.

Write down the length of its diameter.

7. Use a pair of compasses to draw a circle with a radius of 4·5 cm.

Chapter 10

2 Dimensions

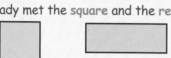
Quadrilaterals

> Be able to recognise Quadrilaterals and know some of their properties

What is meant by "Quadrilateral" ?

A "Quadrilateral" is a closed 4 sided linear shape.

The shape is made up of 4 straight lines.

You have already met the square and the rectangle.

In this chapter we examine their properties and introduce 4 other special quadrilaterals ....

 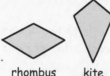

rhombus   kite   parallelogram   trapezium

The Square

Exercise 1

1. Use a ruler to draw a neat square ABCD with sides 5 centimetres.

    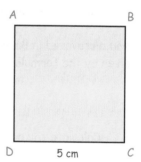

    Answer the following questions about the square :-

    a   Are all four sides the same length ?

    b   Are the opposite pairs of sides parallel ?

    c   Are all four angles the same size ?

    d   How many lines of symmetry has the square ?

    e   Does it have :-   (i) $\frac{1}{2}$ turn symmetry   (ii) $\frac{1}{4}$ turn symmetry ?

    f   If this square was cut out of the page, in how many ways could it fit back in the hole left in the page ?

    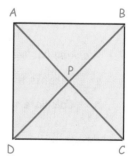

    Now carefully draw in the two diagonals, AC and BD meeting in the middle at P.

    g   Are the two diagonals the same length ?

    h   Does one diagonal bisect the other one (cut it in half) ?

    i   Do the two diagonals cross each other at right angles (is ∠APB = 90°) ?

    j   Does each diagonal bisect the end angle (i.e. does BD cut ∠ADC in half) ?

    (The above are called the properties of a square).

2. The square is the most **perfect** of all quadrilaterals.

Make a list of at least **10 properties** starting with :–

      1.   All 4 sides are the same length.

      2.   Opposite sides are par........

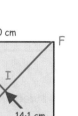

3. Look at square EFGH, shown opposite.

   a   Make a neat **sketch** of it.

   b   Fill in the sizes of all the
        other sides and angles.

4. a   Draw a square, KLMN, with sides 7 centimetres.

   b   Draw in the 2 diagonals, KM and LN, and measure their lengths.

5. a   Draw a square starting with its two diagonals 8 centimetres.
        (*make sure they bisect each other at right angles*)

   b   Measure the lengths of each of the sides of the square.

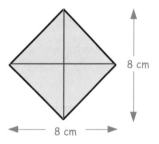

6. a   Draw another square with its diagonals 11 centimetres.

   b   Measure the lengths of each of its sides.

7. a   Draw a square which has a **perimeter** of 24 centimetres.

   b   Measure the lengths of its diagonals.

8. You discovered in **Book 2(a)** that the **area** of a square is
given by the formula :–

$$A = L \times B$$

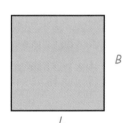

   a   Calculate the **area** of a square with sides 4 cm.

   b   Calculate the **area** of a square with sides 10 cm.

   c   Calculate the **area** of a square with sides 2·5 cm.

   d   Check that the square in Question 5, has an **area** of 32 cm².

9. *Working backwards.* A square has an area of 49 cm².

   a   What is the length of each of its sides ?

   b   Calculate the **perimeter** of this square.

10. Shown are 2 identical squares, PQRS
and RSTU, side by side.

Calculate the size of ∠PSU.

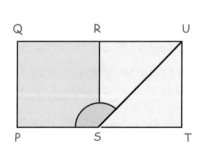

The Rectangle

1. Use a ruler to draw rectangle ABCD
    7 centimetres by 4 centimetres.

    Answer the following questions
    about this rectangle :-

    a   Are all four sides the same length ?

    b   Are **opposite** pairs of sides the same length ?

    c   Are opposite pairs of sides parallel ?

    d   Are all four angles the same size ?

    e   How many lines of symmetry has the rectangle ?

    f   Does it have :-   (i) $\frac{1}{2}$ turn symmetry   (ii) $\frac{1}{4}$ turn symmetry ?

    g   If the rectangle was cut out, in how many ways
         could it be fitted back into the page ?

    Now carefully draw the two diagonals, AC and BD meeting
    in the middle at E.

    h   Are the two diagonals the same length ?

    i   Does one diagonal **bisect** the other one (**cut it in half**) ?

    j   Do the two diagonals cross each other at right angles (is ∠AEB = 90°) ?

    k   Does each diagonal bisect the end angle (is ∠ADE = ∠EDC) ?

         (*The above are called the* ***properties*** *of the rectangle*).

2. Make a list of **5 properties** of a rectangle which make it different from a square.

    Here's one to start you off :-

         1.   The rectangle does **not** have all its four sides the same length.

         2.   ....

3. Look at the rectangular flag shown opposite.

    a   Make a neat **sketch** of the rectangle.

    b   Fill in the sizes of the other
         five lengths.

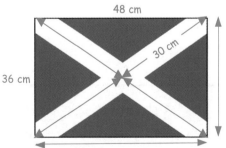

4. a   Neatly and accurately draw a rectangle measuring 8 cm by 6 cm.

    b   Measure the lengths of its 2 diagonals.

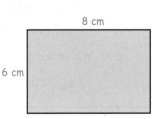

5. Draw a rectangle with its diagonals 8 centimetres long.

> (note 1 :   Start with one diagonal, find its midpoint, and draw the other
>   diagonal through this midpoint).
>
> (note 2 :   Your rectangle may look different from your neighbours).

6. Draw a rectangle with its diagonals 11 centimetres long.

7. a   Draw a rectangle with a **perimeter** of 20 centimetres.

    b   Draw a different rectangle with a **perimeter** of 20 centimetres.

    c   Draw a third rectangle with a **perimeter** of 20 centimetres.

    d   If you start to draw a rectangle with **perimeter** 20 cm and you begin with one of
         its sides 5 cm long, what special type of rectangle will you end up with ?

8. You learned in **Book 2(a)** that the **area** of a rectangle is given by the formula :-

    $$A = L \times B$$

    Calculate the area of a rectangle measuring 7 cm by 3 cm.

9. Calculate the **area** of these rectangles :–

    a    b 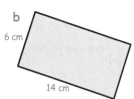   c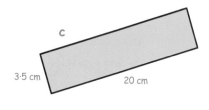

10. Shown is a square ACEG and a rectangle CEJL.

    Calculate the **area** of the whole shape

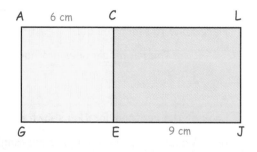

11. Shown is a sketch of a rectangle with a **perimeter** of 24 cm.

    a   Sketch another which also has a perimeter of 24 cm.

    b   Sketch a further 4 rectangles with perimeter 24 cm.

    c   Calculate the **areas** of the 6 rectangles you have sketched.

    d   Which has the **largest** area ?

    e   What **special** kind of rectangle was the one with the largest area ? (*Comment on this*).

The Rhombus (Diamond)

A rhombus has some of the properties of a square but not all of them.

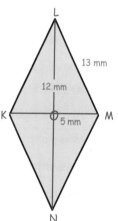

square

rhombus

Exercise 3

1. With a ruler, draw a rhombus with **diagonals** 6 cm and 4 cm.

   Use your figure to answer the following questions about the rhombus :-

   a   Are all four sides the same length ?

   b   Are the **opposite** pairs of sides parallel ?

   c   Are all four angles the same size ?

   d   Are opposite pairs of angles the same size ?
       (∠BAD and ∠BCD)

   e   How many lines of symmetry has the rhombus ?

   f   Does it have :-   **(i)** $\frac{1}{2}$ turn symmetry   **(ii)** $\frac{1}{4}$ turn symmetry ?

   g   If the rhombus was cut out, in how many ways could it be fitted back in the page ?

   Now draw the two diagonals, AC and BD, meeting in the middle at P.

   h   Are the two diagonals the same length ?

   i   Does one diagonal **bisect** the other diagonal ?

   j   Do the two diagonals cross each other at right angles (is ∠BPA = 90°) ?

   k   Does each diagonal bisect the end angle (i.e. is ∠BAP = ∠DAP) ?

       (*The above are called the* **properties** *of a rhombus*).

2. Make a list of **5 properties** of a rhombus which make it different from a square.

   To start you off :-

       1.   The rhombus does **not** have all its 4 **angles** the same size.

       2.   It only has .... lines of symmetry, whereas the square has four.

       3.   ....

3. Look at the rhombus KLMN with LM = 13 mm, LO = 12 mm and OM = 5 mm.

   a   What are the lengths of the sides KL, KN and MN ?

   b   What are the lengths of the lines OK and ON ?

4. The easiest way to draw an accurate rhombus is :-

       – **not** by drawing its four sides first.

       – but by drawing its **two diagonals** first.

The diagram shows how to draw a rhombus PQRS with diagonals 10 cm and 6 cm.

Use the instructions to draw rhombus PQRS.

5. a   Draw rhombus ABCD with

        • diagonal AC = 8 cm
        • diagonal BD = 4 cm.

    b   Measure the length of each of its 4 sides.

6. Draw a rhombus with diagonals 14 cm and 5 cm.

7. a   Draw a rhombus with diagonals 8 cm and 8 cm.

    b   What **special** type of rhombus have you drawn ?

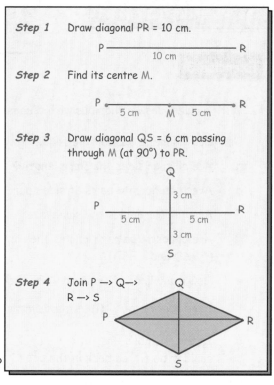

Step 1   Draw diagonal PR = 10 cm.

P ———————————— R
            10 cm

Step 2   Find its centre M.

P •———————•———————• R
   5 cm   M   5 cm

Step 3   Draw diagonal QS = 6 cm passing through M (at 90°) to PR.

Step 4   Join P —> Q—> R —> S

| The Kite |

The paper and string toy flown in the wind is named after this mathematical shape.

Exercise 4

1. Use a ruler to make an accurate drawing of this kite. (or trace it into your jotter).

    Answer these questions about the kite :-

    a   Are all four sides the same length ?

    b   Are **opposite** sides the same length ?

    c   Are there any pairs of equal sides ?

    d   Are the opposite sides parallel ?

    e   Are all four angles the same size ?

    f   Are the top and bottom angles the same size ?

    g   Are the right and left angles the same size ?

    h   How many lines of symmetry has the kite ?

    i   Does it have $\frac{1}{2}$ turn symmetry ?

    j   If the kite was cut out, in how many ways could it be fitted back into the remaining hole ?

Start by drawing the 2 diagonals

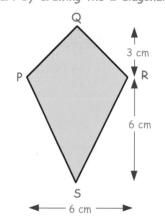

2. Now carefully draw the two diagonals, PR and QS meeting at the point X.

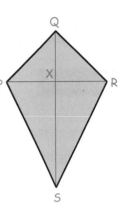

a   Are the two diagonals the same length ?

b   Does diagonal PR bisect QS ?

c   Does diagonal QS bisect PR ?

d   Do the two diagonals cross each other at right angles (is ∠QXP = 90°) ?

e   Does diagonal PR cut the end angles in half (is ∠QRX = ∠SRX) ?

f   Does diagonal QS cut the end angles in half (is ∠PQX = ∠RQX) ?

   (*The above are called the properties of a kite*).

3. Make a list of the properties of a kite which make it different from a square.

   To start you off :-

   1.   The kite does **not** have all its sides the same length.

   2.   Its opposite sides are **not** parallel.

   3.   ....

4. a   Make a neat sketch of kite KLMN
   and mark in the 3 missing lengths.

   b   Copy and complete, using letters :-

   (i)   KL = ...   (ii)   MN = ...

   (iii) OL = ...   (iv)   ∠LKO = ∠......

   (v)   ∠KNO = ∠......   (vi)   ∠LMO = ∠......

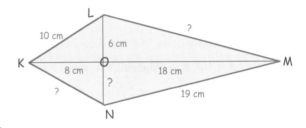

5. Here is kite ABCD, with diagonals of length 12 cm and 8 cm.

   a   If you were asked to draw a kite like this,
      but with line MC = 9 cm, you would end up with
      a "special" type of kite.

      What is the name given to this special type of kite ?

   b   If your kite had MA = MB = MC = MD = 9 cm, what
      special type of kite would you have this time ?

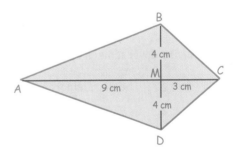

6. This shape consists of 4 identical kites surrounding a central point.

   The blue square surrounding the kites has its sides 30 cm long.

   The smaller diagonal of the kite is 8 cm long.

   Calculate the length of the red dotted line.

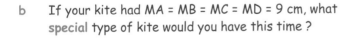

As the name suggests, a parallelogram is a quadrilateral with both pairs of opposite sides parallel.

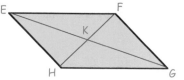

rectangle

parallelogram

a "squashed" rectangle

Exercise 5

1. Use a ruler to make a neat sketch of a parallelogram like EFGH.

    Answer the following questions about the parallelogram :-

    a   Are all four sides the same length ?

    b   Are **opposite** pairs of sides equal ?

    c   Are opposite pairs of sides parallel ?

    d   Are all four angles the same size ?

    e   Are opposite pairs of angles equal (i.e. ∠HEF = ∠FGH) ?

    f   Does it have :-   (i) $\frac{1}{2}$ turn symmetry ?   (ii) $\frac{1}{4}$ turn symmetry ?

    g   How many lines of symmetry does it have (check again) ?

    h   If the parallelogram was cut out of the page, in how
        many ways could it be fitted back into the page ?

    Now carefully draw the two diagonals, EG and FH meeting at K.

    i   Are the two diagonals the same length (Check by measuring) ?

    j   Does each diagonal bisect the other diagonal ?

    k   Do the diagonals meet at right angles (i.e. is ∠EKF = 90°) ?

    l   Does each diagonal cut the end angle in half (i.e. is ∠EFK = ∠GFK) ?

        (*The above are called the properties of the parallelogram*).

2. Write down some **properties** of a parallelogram which make it **different** from a rectangle.

    1.   The parallelogram does **not** have all its angles equal.

    2.   ....

3.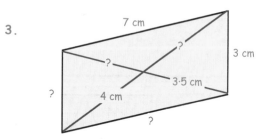

    Make a neat **sketch** of this parallelogram
    and mark in the 4 missing lengths.

4. a   A parallelogram has both its diagonals the same length. What kind of parallelogram is it ?

    b   The diagonals of a parallelogram meet at right angles. What kind of parallelogram is it ?

    c   The diagonals of a parallelogram meet at right angles and both diagonals are the same length.
        What kind of parallelogram is it this time ?

Which Quadrilateral am I ?

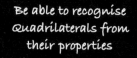

Be able to recognise Quadrilaterals from their properties

Exercise 6

Choose your answers from :-
    Square, Rectangle, Rhombus, Kite or Parallelogram.
    (*Some questions may have more than 1 answer*).

1.   I have 4 equal sides and my 4 angles are 90°.

2.   I have 4 equal sides, but my 4 angles are not 90°.

3.   My diagonals bisect each other, but not at 90°.

4.   I only have 1 line of symmetry.

5.   I have 4 equal sides and have only 2 lines of symmetry.

6.   I have 4 lines of symmetry.

7.   Only 1 pair of my opposite angles are equal.

8.   I have 4 equal sides, but my diagonals are not the same length.

9.   I fit into my outline in exactly 4 ways.

10.   My diagonals meet at 90°, but only one bisects the other.

11.   My diagonals are the same length and cross at 90°.

12.   My opposite end angles are equal but not 90° and my opposite sides are parallel.

13.   My diagonals bisect each other and bisect the end angles, but are not equal.

14.   I don't have half turn symmetry.

15.   My diagonals are equal and bisect my end angles.

16.   My diagonals are equal, but don't meet at 90°.

17.   I have quarter turn symmetry.

18.   My 4 angles are equal, but I only fit into my outline in 2 ways.

19.   I have 2 pairs of equal sides, but my opposite sides are not parallel.

20.   I have 2 lines of symmetry, but they are not my diagonals.

21.   I am often referred to as a "diamond".

22.   Only 1 of my diagonals bisects the other.

23.   I am sometimes referred to as a "squashed rectangle".

24.   There is 6th quadrilateral called a trapezium.
    Find out what it looks like, sketch one and make
    a list of any properties it has.

25.   a   Make a list of at least 4 real life objects that are in the shape of a square.

    b   Repeat for each of the other 5 quadrilaterals.

1. Write down the name of this polygon. ⟶

2. 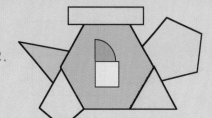 Name all the mathematical shapes you can see in the figure on the left.

3. One of these triangles is isosceles, one is equilateral, the other one is scalene. Which is which ?

   a   b   c

   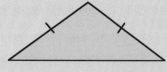

4. Which of the triangles opposite is :-

   a   acute angled

   b   right angled

   c   obtuse angled ?

   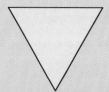

5. 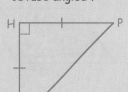 Name and describe this triangle fully.

6. The radius of a circle is 7·5 millimetres. Write down the length of its diameter.

7. Use a pair of compasses and a ruler to draw a semi-circle with a diameter of 10 cm.

8. This shape has three identical semi-circles below a rectangle.

   a   Calculate the length of the diameter of one circle.

   b   What is its radius ?

   c   Now calculate the height (h cm) of the shape.

   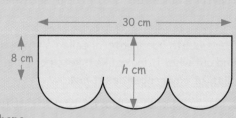

9. What is the name given to these shapes ?

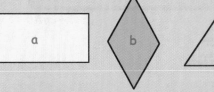 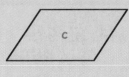 

10. Draw a square with a perimeter of 30 centimetres.

11. A rectangle has sides 6·5 cm and 12 cm.

    a Calculate its perimeter.

    b Calculate its area in cm².

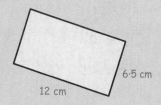

6·5 cm

12 cm

12. a Draw a rhombus with diagonals 12 cm and 5 cm.

    b Measure and write down the length of a side.

13.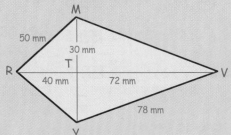

    M

    50 mm

    30 mm

    T

    R   40 mm   72 mm   V

    78 mm

    y

    Look at kite RMVY.

    a What is the length of :-

       (i) TY   (ii) MV   (iii) RY ?

    b Write down an angle equal to :-

       (i) ∠MVT   (ii) ∠YRT.

14. a Make a neat sketch of this parallelogram and mark
       in the four missing lengths.

    b On your diagram, draw in any line of symmetry.

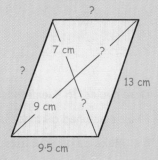

?

7 cm   ?

?

13 cm

9 cm   ?

9·5 cm

15. Here is a list of properties belonging to quadrilaterals.

    Write down which quadrilaterals have these properties. (There may be more than 1 answer).

    a It has four equal sides.

    b It fits its outline in 8 ways.

    c Its opposite sides are parallel.

    d Its diagonals bisect at right angles.

    e Its diagonals bisect the end angles.

    f It has half-turn symmetry.

    g Diagonals bisect each other, but not at 90°.

    h It fits into its outline in only one way.

    i Only one diagonal bisects the other.

Consolidation of Algebra

1. Copy the following and find what * stands for :-

   a 8 + * = 11
      * = ...

   b 15 - * = 7
      * = ...

   c 6 x * = 24
      * = ...

2. What number does ▭ stand for each time here :-

   a 6 + ▭ = 11

   b ▭ x 5 = 30

   c $\frac{▭}{3}$ = 10

   d ▭ - 10 = 9

   e $\frac{42}{▭}$ = 6

   f 17 x ▭ = 0

   g $\frac{▭}{2}$ = 4·5

   h ▭ + 8·5 = 13·6

   i ▭ - 55 = 0 ?

3. In each of the following, the symbol ▬ stands for +, -, x or ÷.
   Decide which symbol is needed each time here :-

   a 7 ▬ 2 = 5

   b 9 ▬ 2 = 18

   c 15 ▬ 3 = 5

   d 9 ▬ 5 = 14

   e 32 ▬ 4 = 8

   f 7 ▬ 2 = 14

   g 4·5 ▬ 4·5 = 9

   h 9 ▬ 9 = 0

   i 7 ▬ 7 = 1.

4. Solve the following equations (find the value of the letter) :-

   a $x + 3 = 17$

   b $x - 3 = 22$

   c $4 \times w = 36$

   d $\frac{p}{7} = 2$

   e $q - 15 = 15$

   f $55 \div g = 5$.

5. Dave cycles 26 kilometres and Eric cycles * kilometres.

   Their combined distance is 55 kilometres.

   a Make up an equation using *.

   b Solve it to find how far Eric cycled.

6.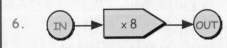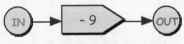

   Machine A   Machine B

   a What number comes out when :-

      (i) 7 is put into machine A

      (ii) 23 is put into machine B ?

   b What number has gone in when :-

      (i) 32 comes out of machine A

      (ii) 26 comes out of machine B ?

Chapter 11

Number Machines

Use a number machine to follow instructions involving two calculations

Remember :-

A number machine (or function machine) is the name for a mathematical rule which changes one number into another.

Sometimes this rule can involve two or more processes.

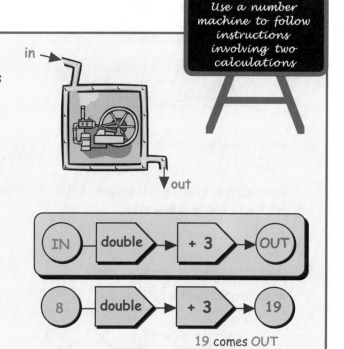

Example :-   This number machine takes a number **IN** one side **doubles it** then adds 3 and pushes the answer **OUT** the other side.

The number 8 is put **IN** :-

19 comes **OUT**

Exercise 1

1.   Look again at the function machine above.

   a   What comes **out** when you put **in** the number :-

   (i)   1   (ii)   10   (iii)   25   (iv)   2·3   (v)   0 ?

   b   What number must have been put **in** to produce the answer :-

   (i)   9   (ii)   27   (iii)   333   (iv)   9·6   (v)   21·8 ?

2.   Here is a new function machine.

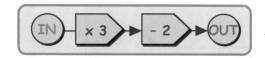

   a   What comes **out** of this machine when you put **in** the number :-

   (i)   9   (ii)   12   (iii)   8·5   (iv)   40   (v)   0·8 ?

   b   What number must have been put **in** to produce the answer :-

   (i)   16   (ii)   43   (iii)   34   (iv)   2·5   (v)   298 ?

3.   Look at these number machines. Write down what number comes **OUT** :-

   a   b

3.
c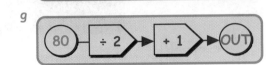

d

e

f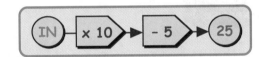

g

h

4.   Here is another number machine.

(Read the question carefully).

What number must have been put IN to
get the following numbers OUT :-

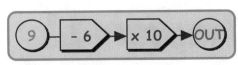

   a   5 (*the answer is NOT 9*)   b   17   c   29   d   20 ?

5.   Look at the number machines below.

What number must have been put IN :-

a

b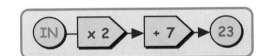

c

d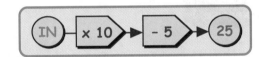

e

f

6.   Write down the missing number (or sign) in each machine below :-

a

b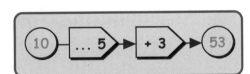

c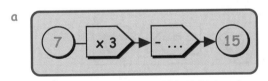

d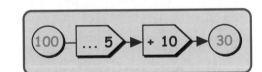

7.   Write down five different sets of signs and
     numbers to make this number machine produce
     the output 25 when 100 is put in.

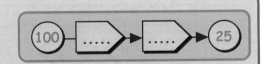

Solving (Basic) Equations

Be able to solve a basic equation

Remember we can solve equations by *cover up* (using a finger).

$x + 5 = 9$
$x = 4$

$p - 3 = 12$
$p = 15$

$y - 7 = 1$
$y = 8$

We can also use our *cover up* method for these type of equations :-

$3x$ means 3 times x.

$3x = 12$
$x = 4$

$2k = 10$
$k = 5$

$7y = 56$
$y = 8$

There are various other ways of solving equations :-

· the "cover up" method $3 \times$ $= 12$

· the method of "equal addition"

· the "change side <—> change sign" rule.

You may come across these alternative methods later.

Exercise 2

1. Copy and solve each equation by finding the value of the letter :-

    a $x + 3 = 7$ b $x + 9 = 12$ c $x + 1 = 17$

    d $y + 11 = 21$ e $y - 3 = 6$ f $y - 1 = 21$

    g $p - 10 = 0$ h $p - 50 = 10$ i $p + 6 = 6$

    j $k - 18 = 0$ k $h + 15 = 30$ l $g - 40 = 40$

    m $5 - q = 1$ n $8 + w = 11$ o $9 - z = 0$

    p $15 + x = 50$ q $17 - r = 14$ r $55 + t = 55$

    s $71 + f = 111$ t $145 - x = 77$ u $515 + y = 761.$

2. Copy each equation and find the value of the letter :-

    a $3x = 6$ b $4m = 20$ c $5p = 30$

    d $7q = 28$ e $6t = 36$ f $6a = 60$

    g $3b = 36$ h $8d = 48$ i $2x = 24$

    j $2p = 22$ k $4p = 56$ l $6m = 54$

    m $10x = 110$ n $8t = 64$ o $14p = 42$

    p $2b = 5$ q $2c = 9$ r $2n = 19$

    s $4x = 10$ t $8x = 12$ u $10x = 55$

    v $4x = 21$ w $10x = 34$ x $5x = 24.$

Solving Equations

Harder Equations :-

Look at these equations which involve both addition/subtraction and multiplication.

Example 1 :-

$$2x + 1 = 7$$
$$2x = 6$$
$$x = 3$$

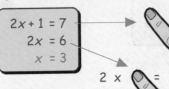

$\boxed{} + 1 = 7$

Ask yourself - "what", add 1, gives 7 ?
The answer is 6 => this means $2x = 6$

$2 \times \boxed{} = 6$

Now ask yourself - 2 times "what", gives 6 ?
The answer is 3 => this means $x = 3$

Can you see we can still use the cover up method ?   *Examples :-*

Discuss each of these examples with your teacher.

$$3x - 2 = 25$$
$$3x = 27$$
$$x = 9$$

$$4x - 6 = 6$$
$$4x = 12$$
$$x = 3$$

Exercise 3

1. Find the value of x by solving each equation below.
   Copy and complete :-

   a
   $$2x + 5 = 11$$
   $$2x = 6$$
   $$x = ...$$

   b
   $$3x + 1 = 13$$
   $$3x = ...$$
   $$x = ...$$

   c
   $$4x - 5 = 15$$
   $$4x = ...$$
   $$x = ...$$

2. Find the value of x by solving these equations :-
   Set down your working carefully.

   a $2x + 3 = 5$ b $3x + 6 = 21$ c $4x + 7 = 23$

   d $5x + 2 = 42$ e $2x - 4 = 6$ f $3x - 3 = 24$

   g $4x - 1 = 35$ h $3x - 6 = 0$ i $6x - 1 = 53$

   j $7x - 2 = 68$ k $8x + 4 = 28$ l $9x - 2 = 61$

   m $2x - 12 = 2$ n $4x + 10 = 22$ o $5x + 20 = 20$

   p $3x - 5 = 55$ q $7x - 7 = 0$ r $2x - 5 = 0$

   s $5x - 1 = 24$ t $2x + 5 = 12$ u $6x - 3 = 12.$

3. Look at the picture showing 2 rods end to end.

   x cm   8 cm

   a   Write down an expression, in terms of x, for the total length of the 2 rods.

   b   Given that the total length of the rods is actually 21 centimetres :-

   (i)   make up an equation involving x.

   (ii) solve it to find the value of x.

4.   Tony has £8 and David has £x. Together they have £17.

a   Make up an equation using this information.

b   Now solve it to determine how much David has.

5.   There were x marbles in a bag. 7 were removed.
I then found that there were 14 left.

a   Make up an equation about the marbles.

b   Now solve it to determine how many there
were to begin with.

6.   For each of the following :–   (i) make an equation and   (ii) solve it.

a   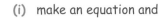   Chad has x pencils in his case. Harry has 14 pencils.

Altogether they have 31 pencils.

b   Eliose has to cycle 2·3 kilometres to school.
Franz has to walk y kilometres.

They travel a total of 3·1 kilometres.

c   Tom cycles from his house to the park then
to the beach, a total of 34 kilometres.

From his house to the park is 20 km.

The park to the beach is p kilometres.

7.   To find the area of a rectangle you **multiply** its length by its breadth.

a   Write down an expression for the
area of this rectangle in terms of x.

b   If the actual area is 24 cm^2,

(i)   write down an equation involving x,

(ii)   solve it to find the value of x.

4 cm

x cm

8.   Find the value of x in each case :-

a $\frac{1}{2}x = 7$ b $\frac{1}{3}x = 9$ c $\frac{1}{4}x = 20$

d $\frac{1}{5}x = 10$ e $\frac{1}{10}x = 5$ f $\frac{1}{8}x = 2$

g $\frac{1}{6}x = 11$ h $\frac{1}{5}x = 20$ i $\frac{1}{2}x = 3\frac{1}{2}$

j $\frac{1}{2}x + 1 = 6$ k $\frac{1}{3}x - 4 = 2$ l $\frac{1}{4}x - 2 = 1$

m $\frac{1}{2}x - 2 = 1$ n $\frac{1}{5}x + 1 = 3$ o $\frac{1}{10}x - 10 = 10.$

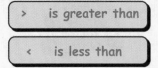

Be able to interpret and write an inequality

The equations you were solving were called **equations** because they each had the "=" sign in them.

There are 4 other mathematical signs, called **inequalities** and they are :-

> | is greater than   ≥ | is greater than or equal to

< | is less than   ≤ | is less than or equal to

Examples :-

  5 > 3   "five is greater than three"

  -7 < -6   "negative seven is less than negative six"

  $x ≥ 2$ "*x* is greater than or equal to two"   (*x* can be 2 or any number above 2)

  $y ≤ -5$ "*y* is less than or equal to negative five"   (*y* can be –5 or any number below –5).

Have you noticed ??   -   The arrow (<), (>) always points to the **smaller** number.

7 > 3   -6 < -4

smaller

smaller

Exercise 4

1.   COPY the following as shown and place a "<" sign or a ">" sign between the numbers :-

  a   8 ... 1   b   2 ... 5   c   0 ... -5

  d   -4 ... -3   e   6 ... -3   f   -8 ... -17

  g   -117 ... -116   h   -141 ... -140   i $12 ... 11\frac{1}{2}$.

2.   Rewrite the following pairs of numbers to suit the given sign :-

  Example :- write 5 and 4 using a "<" sign.   =>   answer is :- 4 < 5.

  a   8 and 3, using "<"   b   8 and 3, using ">"   c   17 and 11, using "<"

  d   -8 and -5, using ">"   e   -2 and 2, using ">"   f   5 and -1 using, "<"

  g   -15 and -14, using "<"   h   -77 and -79, using ">"   i   9 and -10 using, "<".

3.   In this question you must choose *x* only from the numbers ..... 0, 1, 2, 3, or 4.

  Examples :-   (i) $x ≥ 1$ gives *x* = 1, 2, 3, 4.   (ii) $x < 3$ gives *x* = 0, 1, 2.

  a $x > 2$ b $x < 4$ c $x ≥ 3$

  d $x ≤ 1$ e $x > 0$ f $x ≤ 4$

  g $x > 4$ h $x ≥ 0$ i $x ≤ 0$.

4. In this question you must choose y only from the numbers, $-3, -2, -1, 0, 1, 2, 3$.

    a $y > 1$ b $y < 0$ c $y \geq -1$

    d $y \leq 1$ e $y > -3$ f $y \leq -2$

    g $y > -2$ h $y < 1$ i $y \geq -3$.

5. For each of the following given statements, make up your own inequality :-

    > *Example :-* the **maximum** crowd (C) at Hampden Park is set at 52 000.
    >
    > => $C \leq 52\,000$

    a   The maximum permitted crowd (C) at Fir Park is set at 14 000.

    => C ....

    b   Voters have to be 18 years old or over.

        (i)   Brian is Y years old and **can** vote. => $Y \geq$ .....

        (ii) Paula is T years old and cannot vote. => .....

    c   The maximum number of passengers on a bus is 51.
        There were P people on the bus. => .....

    d   The speed limit outside school buildings is now 20 mph.
        Cheryl was booked for speeding outside a school.
        She was travelling at V mph. => .....

    e   A child's pedal car race has a maximum speed limit of 12 mph.
        The car was travelling at S miles per hour. => .....

    f   A group booking for a Paintball competition needs to be a minimum of 6.
        Andi is booking his group of Y people. => .....

    g   The cost of a train season ticket is £40. Beryl has £M.
        She has got enough money with her to buy one. => .....

    h   To win a penalty competition Nick requires to score at least 6 penalties.
        He didn't win ! He scored P penalties. => .....

    i   In a Maths test out of 20, a mark of 16 or more was regarded as a GREAT pass.
        Charles got a GREAT pass. He scored M marks out of 20. => .....

    j   To heat pies in an oven requires the oven to be set at 220°C for 30 minutes.
        Sally had put pies in the oven for 30 minutes but had totally burned them.
        The oven temperature for the 30 minutes was T (°C). => .....

    k   A computer game costs £40.
        Mary has £x. Sid has £y. By putting their money together they find that
        they have **more** than enough to buy the game. => .....

Solving Further Inequalities

To solve an **inequality**, you use the same technique used to solve an equation.

Look at the this **example** :-

Comparing the equation $\quad \boxed{\begin{array}{l} x + 5 = 9 \\ \quad x = 4 \end{array}}$ to the inequality $\quad \boxed{\begin{array}{l} x + 5 < 9 \\ \quad x < 4 \end{array}}$

note

Here are 3 further **examples** :-

$\boxed{\begin{array}{l} x - 5 > 6 \\ \quad x > 11 \end{array}}$ $\qquad$ $\boxed{\begin{array}{l} x + 4 > 10 \\ \quad x > 6 \end{array}}$ $\qquad$ $\boxed{\begin{array}{l} x - 2 \geq 5 \\ \quad x \geq 7 \end{array}}$

Exercise 5

1. Solve these **inequalities**, leaving your answers in the form :- $x > 3$, $x < 5$, $x \geq -1$, etc.

   a $\quad x + 1 > 5$ $\qquad$ b $\quad x + 2 > 11$ $\qquad$ c $\quad x + 8 \leq 9$

   d $\quad x + 7 < 15$ $\qquad$ e $\quad x - 1 \leq 8$ $\qquad$ f $\quad x - 5 \geq 20$

   g $\quad x - 10 > 0$ $\qquad$ h $\quad x - 20 < 50$ $\qquad$ i $\quad x + 7 \leq 7$

   j $\quad x - 8 \geq 0$ $\qquad$ k $\quad x + 59 < 60$ $\qquad$ l $\quad x - 40 > 40$

   m $\quad x + 3 \cdot 1 < 4 \cdot 2$ $\qquad$ n $\quad x - 111 > 99$ $\qquad$ o $\quad x + \frac{1}{2} < 1$

   p $\quad 11 + x > 13$ $\qquad$ q $\quad 3 + x \geq 10$ $\qquad$ r $\quad 21 + x < 25$.

Inequalities like "$4x < 24$" are tackled the same way as the **equivalent equation**.

Examples :-

$\boxed{\begin{array}{l} 3x > 12 \\ \quad x > 4 \end{array}}$ $\qquad$ $\boxed{\begin{array}{l} 6x < 12 \\ \quad x \leq 2 \end{array}}$ $\qquad$ $\boxed{\begin{array}{l} 7x \geq 42 \\ \quad x \geq 6 \end{array}}$

2. Solve each inequality, leaving your answers in the form :- $x > 3$, $x < 5$, $x \geq -1$, etc.

   a $\quad 3x < 21$ $\qquad$ b $\quad 4x > 20$ $\qquad$ c $\quad 5x < 55$

   d $\quad 6x \geq 54$ $\qquad$ e $\quad 7x \leq 49$ $\qquad$ f $\quad 8x > 80$

   g $\quad 8x < 40$ $\qquad$ h $\quad 10x \leq 100$ $\qquad$ i $\quad 3x > 0$

   j $\quad 11x \geq 11$ $\qquad$ k $\quad 3x < 9$ $\qquad$ l $\quad 12x > 36$

   m $\quad 2x > 4 \cdot 6$ $\qquad$ n $\quad 18x \leq 180$ $\qquad$ o $\quad 14x \geq 1400$

   p $\quad 3x < 2400$ $\qquad$ q $\quad 5x > 1250$ $\qquad$ r $\quad 5x \leq 120$.

3. For each of the following given statements, make up your own **inequality** and solve it to find x :-

a Gary has £x saved. Josh has £120.

Together they **do not** have enough money to buy a game station costing £190. => x .....

(*hint* :- $x +$ .... < 190)

b Vera and Sara are saving together for a holiday, total cost £775.

Vera has £x and Sara has £400. They have **more** than enough saved. => .....

c James has £x in his bank. He withdraws £10.

He still has **more** than enough in his account to pay for a bank charge of £35. => => .....

d Sally has £x. Brenda has twice as much as Sally.

Brenda has less than £50. => .....

e The maximum speed limit in a village is x mph.

Darren received a ticket for going at 2 times the speed limit.

Darren was travelling faster than 60 mph. => .....

4. Find the value of x by solving these inequalities :- (*Set down your working carefully*).

a	$3x + 2 < 14$	b	$2x + 5 > 13$	c	$5x + 1 < 1$
d	$4x + 2 \geq 34$	e	$6x - 1 \leq 23$	f	$5x - 16 > 39$
g	$8x - 8 \leq 0$	h	$4x - 6 < 6$	i	$9x - 2 > 52$
j	$10x - 3 \geq 57$	k	$7x + 10 < 45$	l	$6x - 11 \leq 55$
m	$5x - 12 \geq 3$	n	$9x + 10 < 10$	o	$2x + 7 \geq 12$
p	$\frac{1}{2}x - 12 \geq 3$	q	$\frac{1}{2}x + 10 < 10$	r	$0{\cdot}1x + 7 \geq 12.$

5. Solve each inequality, by taking each value from the given list and checking to see if it works :-

	Inequality	*Numbers chosen from*		*Inequality*	*Numbers chosen from*
a	$2x > 6$	{1, 2, 3, 4, 5}	b	$4x < 20$	{1, 2, 3, 4, 5}
c	$x + 4 < 7$	{0, 1, 2, 3, 4}	d	$x - 5 > 0$	{2, 3, 4, 5, 6, 7}
e	$4x + 2 \geq 6$	{0, 1, 2, 3}	f	$3x - 1 \leq 8$	{-1, 0, 1, 2, 3, 4}
g	$15 - x \geq 12$	{1, 2, 3, 4, 5, 6}	h	$15 - 2x \leq 11$	{0, 1, 2, 3, 4, 5, 6}
i	$3x > 3$	{-1, 0, 1, 2, 3}	j	$\frac{1}{2}x \leq 1$	{-2, -1, 0, 1, 2, 3, 4, 5}.

Revisit - Review - Revise

1. a What number must have gone into this number machine ?

b What number should come out of this number machine ?

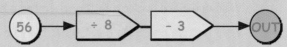

2. Write the sign (+, –, ÷, x) that ◯ stands for each time here :-

a 9 ◯ 3 = 6   b 9 ◯ 3 = 3   c 9 ◯ 3 = 12

3. Solve these equations to find the value of x.

a $x + 3 = 11$ b $x - 5 = 5$ c $x + 15 = 25$

d $x - 7 = 0$ e $2x = 22$ f $\frac{1}{3}x = 6$.

4. There were 30 people on a train. After x people got off there were 21 left on the train.

a Make up an equation about the people on the train.

b Solve the equation to find how many people must have got off.

5. Last week, George earned £x as a barber.

This week he earned double that amount plus tips of £40.

In fact, George earned £440 this week.

Make an equation about using x and solve it to find out how much George must have earned last week.

6. Copy the following and place a "<" sign or a ">" sign between the numbers as appropriate :-

a 21 23   b 13 .... –11   c –212 .... –210.

7. Make up an inequality for the statement below :-

"To drive the Dodgem Cars, you must be at least 130 cm tall".

Laura, who is x cm tall is not allowed to drive a Dodgem Car.

=> x ....

8. In this question you can choose x only from the numbers ..... {–3, –2, –1, 0, 1, 2, 3}

Write down the solutions for :-

a $x > -1$ b $x < -2$ c $x \leq 0$ d $x > -\frac{1}{4}$.

9. Solve the following inequalities, leaving your answer in the form e.g. $x > 2$, $x \leq 3$, etc.

a $x + 5 > 11$ b $x - 7 < 13$ c $6x \leq 24$ d $2x + 5 \geq 21$.

Consolidation of Fractions/Decimals/Percentages

1. For each shape, say what fraction has been coloured :-

   a   b 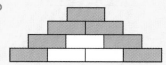   c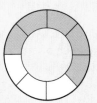

2. For each shape in question 1, write down the fraction **not** coloured.

3. Copy and complete :-

   a $\dfrac{1}{4} = \dfrac{?}{20}$ b $\dfrac{3}{7} = \dfrac{9}{?}$ c $\dfrac{13}{?} = \dfrac{52}{60}$.

4. Write down **two** fractions equivalent to :-

   a $\dfrac{1}{6}$ b $\dfrac{5}{8}$ c $\dfrac{3}{10}$.

5. Write each of these fractions in their **simplest** form :-

   a $\dfrac{5}{15}$ b $\dfrac{18}{24}$ c $\dfrac{50}{75}$.

6. Find :-

   a $\dfrac{1}{4}$ of £36   b $\dfrac{1}{10}$ of 500 m   c $\dfrac{1}{7}$ of \$84.

7. Billy had 24 silver coins in his pocket.
   He found a **quarter** were 50p coins, a **third** were 20p
   coins, a **sixth** were 10p coins and the rest were 5p coins.

   a How many 50p coins did Billy have ?

   b How many 10p coins ?

   c How much money did Billy have altogether ?

8. Find :-

   a $\dfrac{2}{3}$ of £27   b $\dfrac{3}{7}$ of \$280   c $\dfrac{7}{8}$ of £2400.

9. On an army base there were 150 new recruits.

   After a week, $\dfrac{1}{5}$ of them came down with a sickness bug.

   One week later, $\dfrac{2}{3}$ of the **remaining** recruits became sick.

   How many of the original 150 recruits had **not** become sick ?

10. Write down each
    colour as a
    percentage of
    the shape shown :-

11. Write each of the following as a fraction :-

    a 21%   b 39%   c 11%   d 37%
    e 1%   f 9%   g 19%   h 25%.

12. Write each of the following as a decimal :-

    a 43%   b 13%   c 29%   d 9%
    e 5%   f 50%   g 125%   h 1%.

13. Write each of the following as a fraction and as a decimal :-

    a 17%   b 69%   c 3%   d 30%
    e 70%   f 50%   g 25%   h 10%.

14. Write each fraction or decimal as a percentage :-

    a $\frac{79}{100}$ b 0·67   c $\frac{57}{100}$ d 0·01
    e 0·09   f $\frac{3}{100}$ g 0·9   h 1·7.

15. Find :-

    a 50% of 30p   b 25% of 36 mm   c 50% of £15   d 10% of 7 m
    e 25% of 1 kg   f 10% of £11   g 50% of 5 km   h 25% of 110 cm.

You may use a calculator for questions 7 & 8, but you must show working.

16. Find :-

    a 77% of £800   b 51% of 1200 km c 19% of £780   d 3% of £7.

17 a A survey was conducted and 20 000 pupils were asked how they travelled to school.

       60% walked 15% took a bus or train and the rest arrived by car.

       How many pupils :-   (i)   walked   (ii) took a bus   (iii) arrived by car ?

    b    A glider was being flown at a height of 1500 feet.
                                 The glider's height dropped by 40%.

                                 (i)   By how many feet had the glider dropped ?

                                 (ii) At what height was the glider then flying ?

Chapter 12

Reducing a Percentage to a Fraction in its Simplest Form

Be able to reduce a percentage to a fraction in simplest form

Remember $10\% = \dfrac{10}{100}$.

Divide top and bottom by 10 => $\dfrac{10}{100} \begin{smallmatrix} \div 10 \\ \div 10 \end{smallmatrix} = \dfrac{1}{10}$ (its *simplest form*).

Example :-   Reduce each of these percentages to fractions (in *simplest form*).

a   20%   b   50%   c   22%

$$20\% = \frac{20}{100}$$
$$\quad = \frac{1}{5}$$

$$50\% = \frac{50}{100}$$
$$\quad = \frac{5}{10}$$
$$\quad = \frac{1}{2}$$

$$22\% = \frac{22}{100}$$
$$\quad = \frac{11}{50}$$

Exercise 1

1. Reduce each percentage to a fraction in its **simplest form** (where possible) :-

a 25%	b 30%	c 15%	d 23%
e 2%	f 9%	g 95%	h 75%
i 5%	j 34%	k 66%	l 64%
m 40%	n 60%	o 80%	p 27%.

2. Find out which percentages match up with which fractions :-

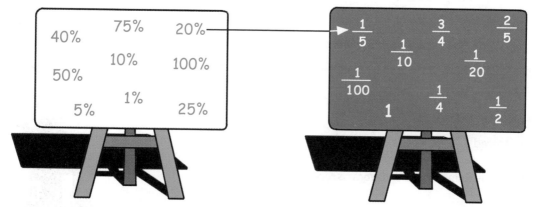

3. Make a copy of this table and complete it :-

percentage	100%	75%	50%	25%	20%	10%	5%	1%
fraction	?	?	$\frac{1}{2}$	?	?	?	?	?

It is now possible for you to do (some) percentage calculations without a calculator.

4. Remember :- 25% means $\frac{1}{4}$. Find, without a calculator :-

    a   25% of £48   (= $\frac{1}{4}$ of 48 = 48 ÷ 4 = £....)

    b   25% of 200 kg   c   25% of £1·20   d   25% of 5200 km.

5. Now try these (use your answers to question 3 to help you) :-

    a   50% of £16   b   20% of £45   c   10% of £82

    d   1% of 600 mm   e   5% of $600   f   100% of £2·50

    g   75% of £40   h   75% of £1·60   i   75% of £800.

It is easier to put fractions, decimals and percentages in order when you reduce each to a percentage.

Example :– Write this list of values in order (largest first) :–   42%, $\frac{2}{5}$, 0·45, $\frac{3}{7}$.

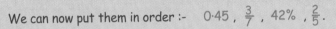

$$\frac{2}{5} = 2 \div 5 = 0.4 \quad = \quad 40\% \qquad 42\% \quad = \quad 42\%$$

$$\frac{3}{7} = 3 \div 7 = 0.43 \quad = \quad 43\% \qquad 0.45 \quad = \quad 45\%$$

We can now put them in order :–   0·45, $\frac{3}{7}$, 42%, $\frac{2}{5}$.

---

6. Write each of the lists below in order (largest first) :-

    a   77%, $\frac{79}{100}$, 0·8, 0·78   b   22%, $\frac{2}{5}$, 0·3, $\frac{8}{31}$, 0·225

    c $\frac{3}{11}$, 0·24, 29%, $\frac{2}{9}$ d $\frac{1}{3}$, $\frac{2}{7}$, $\frac{3}{10}$, $\frac{4}{11}$, $\frac{7}{26}$.

7. a   Write down any five fractions of your own. Rearrange these in order (smallest first).

    b   Hand the fractions to a neighbour and time him/her to see how long it takes to arrange them.

8. Ralph sat four exams.

    He scored $\frac{71}{100}$ in Maths, $\frac{7}{10}$ in English, $\frac{9}{12}$ in French and $\frac{22}{30}$ in Music.

    What was Ralph's best and worst score ?

9. In a special lottery prize Darren was offered one of the following :-

    (i)   40% of £9000   (ii) $\frac{3}{5}$ of £7000   (iii) 0·15 of £20 000.

    Which should he choose ? Explain why.

Calculating a Percentage without a Calculator

Be able to calculate most percentages of a quantity without a calculator

You now have some percentages that can be reduced into simple fractions for calculations **without** using a calculator.

But there are many percentages that can be calculated **without** a calculator.

Examples :-

a | Find 3% of ...
- Find 1%
- then times by 3.

b | Find 70% of ...
- Find 10%
- then times by 7.

c | Find 11% of ....
- Find 10%, find 1% then
- add your two answers.

Exercise 2

1. Make a copy of the list shown below and LEARN it :-

percentage	50%	25%	75%	$33\frac{1}{3}$ %	$66\frac{2}{3}$ %	20%	40%	60%	80%	10%	30%	70%	90%
fraction	$\frac{1}{2}$	$\frac{1}{4}$	$\frac{3}{4}$	$\frac{1}{3}$	$\frac{2}{3}$	$\frac{1}{5}$	$\frac{2}{5}$	$\frac{3}{5}$	$\frac{4}{5}$	$\frac{1}{10}$	$\frac{3}{10}$	$\frac{7}{10}$	$\frac{9}{10}$

note   note

2. Do the following by using the fractional equivalents instead of the percentages :-

a   10% of £120
b   20% of £120
c   40% of £120

d   10% of £40
e   5% of £40 (half of 10%)
f   75% of £240

g $33\frac{1}{3}$ % of £15
h $66\frac{2}{3}$ % of £15
i   25% of £140

j   30% of £14
k   20% of £760
l   60% of £350

m $33\frac{1}{3}$ % of £9·30
n $66\frac{2}{3}$ % of £9·30
o   50% of £3

p   75% of £36
q   10% of £180
r   5% of £180

s   1% of £700
t   2% of £700
u   3% of £700

v   75% of £480
w $33\frac{1}{3}$ % of £3900
x   5% of £120

y $66\frac{2}{3}$ % of £4·50
z   11% of £30.

3. Harder !! (no calculator). Discuss how, without a calculator, you might find :-

a   15% of something
b $2\frac{1}{2}$ % of something
c $17\frac{1}{2}$ % of something ?

4. Find :-

a   15% of £80
b   15% of 160 km

c $2\frac{1}{2}$ % of 1400 km
d $2\frac{1}{2}$ % of £4
e $17\frac{1}{2}$ % of 480 ml

f $17\frac{1}{2}$ % of £640
g $17\frac{1}{2}$ % of £8
h   17·5% of 1480 ml

i $22\frac{1}{2}$ % of 1600 mm
j   22·5% of 80 cm
k   7·5% of 1200 litres.

CfE Book 2b - Chapter 12   this is page 123   Fractions, Decimals & Percentages

1.   A school has 420 pupils. 10% of the pupils are on a trip.

How many pupils are there on the trip ?

2.   Five hundred and twenty trees are planted in a town.
20% of them are planted in a park.

How many trees are planted in the park ?

3.   A recipe requires 680 g of flour.

25% of the flour is self-raising.

How much of the flour is self-raising ?

4.   The Cat and Dog home have 114 animals. $33\frac{1}{3}$ % are cats.

How many cats are there ?

5.   a   Abbie had £220. She spent 25% on an weekend spa break.

How much did Abbie pay for her break ?

   b   Ellie weighed 85 kilograms.
She went to a health resort for a week and lost 20% of her weight.

(i)   How many kilograms did she lose ?

(ii)   How much does she weigh after her visit to the health resort ?

   c   Dara paid a 75% deposit on a £380 mountain bike.

How much was his deposit ?

   d   Arnie does 150 sit-ups every day.
He does 60% in the morning and the rest at night.

(i)   How many sit-ups does he do in the morning ?

(ii)   What percentage of the sit-ups does he do at night ?

   e   75% of the animals in a farm yard are chickens.

If there are 96 animals in the yard, how many are not chickens ?

6.   a   The price tag on a jacket reads £60. It also carries a $33\frac{1}{3}$ % discount label.
How much will the jacket now cost ?

   b   Gary received a 5% discount on his £1800 car. How much did Gary pay for his car ?

7.   Zeus Clothing is offering a $12\frac{1}{2}$ % discount on all items.
How much will it cost for :-   a   a coat priced £120   b   a watch costing £48 ?

You may use a calculator for questions 8 - 12.

8. a   A bank charges 14% for a £6400 car loan.
        How much did the bank charge for the loan ?

$$\frac{14}{100} \times 6400$$

$$= 14 \div 100 \times 6400$$

    b   Only 55% of bugs are killed by a bug spray.

        If there were 8600 bugs, how many were killed ?

    c   Hayley's council tax last year was £960. This year there is a 7% increase.
        How much is the increase ?

    d   Last month a house was valued at £120 000.
        This month the house is valued at 3·5% less.

        How much less is the value of the house ?

9.    The storm yesterday had winds of 60 mph.
                           The wind speed is expected to increase by 15% today.

                           What is the expected wind speed today ?

10. a   A bus service is to increase its Zone Card price by 11%.

        How much will I pay for my £28 Zone Card after the increase ?

    b   A bus driver gets a pay rise of 6%.

        How much will a bus driver earning £325 a week now earn ?

    c   Tyre pressure on a bus should be at 56 p.s.i. (*pounds per square inch*).

        If the pressure drops by 25%, what would the p.s.i. be ?

11. a   Avia offers a 17·5% discount on their hire cars.

        How much would it cost to hire a car originally costing £124 ?

    b   A garage has a car priced £12 800 for sale.
        The *Managers Special* discount is 7·25%.

        How much will the car cost with the *special* discount ?

12. a   A pick-up truck was given a 10% discount and was sold for £9000.
        How much was the pick-up before the discount ? (not £9900) !

    b      TravelCo gave a 5% discount and sold a week in Malta for £190.

                               How much was the holiday before the discount ?

    c   After spending 75% of his savings on a trip, Ed still had £1000 left.

        What was his original savings before the trip ?

    d   Ally had £2000 left of his lottery win after spending 80% of his money.

        How much did he win on the lottery ?

The 3 Я's

Revisit - Review - Revise

1. What fraction of each shape is red ?

   a 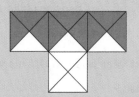   b   c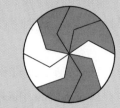

2. Three fifths of the sweets in a packet are mints. What fraction are NOT mints ?

3. a Copy the rectangle shown (4 boxes by 25 boxes).

   COPY

   b Colour 15% of your rectangle blue.

   c Colour 0·2 of your rectangle red.   d Colour $\frac{2}{5}$ of your rectangle yellow.

   e What is the total percentage coloured ?   e What percentage is NOT coloured ?

4. Write down two equivalent fractions to :-   a $\frac{1}{3}$ b $\frac{3}{5}$.

5. Write these as fractions in simplest form :-   a $\frac{24}{36}$ b 35% .

6. Write each fraction or decimal as a percentage :-

   a $\frac{20}{50}$ b 0·73   c $\frac{1}{10}$ d 0·7.

7. Find :-

   a $\frac{2}{5}$ of £24   b $\frac{4}{9}$ of 54 cm   c 20% of 35 litres   d $66\frac{2}{3}$% of 18.

8. Put these in order starting with the smallest :-   22% $\frac{2}{5}$ 0·2.

- -

You may use a calculator for questions 9 - 12.   ✓

9. Write these fractions as percentages :-   a $\frac{3}{4}$ b $\frac{3}{20}$

10. Calculate :-   a 32% of £8760   b 87% of 1800 km   c 3·5% of £6.

11. Write these in order, largest first :- $\frac{5}{9}$, 0·59, 57%, 0·6.

12. a Daphne scored 17 out 25 in a quiz. What percentage did she score ?

    b Sarri is given a 37% discount on a £12 500 car. How much did Sarri pay for his car ?

    c Ina was given a 7·5% discount on a dress costing £112. How much did she pay ?

    d Grace spent 90% of this week's wage and had £35 left. How much was her wage ?

Consolidation of Measurement

LENGTH

1. Use your ruler to measure the length of these lines, in millimetres.

   a ——————————————————— b

2. Write down the lengths of the following lines in :-

   (i) millimetres   (ii) centimetres   (iii) centimetres and millimetres.

   a   b

3. Draw a line 10·5 centimetres long.

4. Change :-

a	3 m to cm	b	12 cm to mm	c	1·8 km to m
d	6000 m to km	e	270 cm to m	f	120 mm to cm
g	4700 m to km	h	2 m 95 cm to cm	i	20·2 metres to cm
j	$3\frac{1}{2}$ metres to cm	k	11·7 cm to mm	l	605 cm to m.

5. A sheet of A4 paper is 29·7 cm long. A strip 30 mm is cut off.

   What is the length of the remaining piece of paper, in millimetres ?

6. Calculate the perimeter
   of this shape :-

   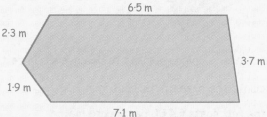

   6·5 m

   2·3 m

   3·7 m

   1·9 m

   7·1 m

7.

   19 cm

   The perimeter of this rectangle is 52 cm.

   Calculate the length of the shorter side .

8. A jeweller makes a pendant in the shape of an isosceles triangle.

   She wishes to surround the pendant with silver wire.

   The silver wire costs £4·00 per centimetre.

   How much will it cost the jeweller to do this ?

   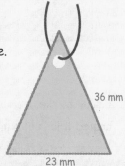

   36 mm

   23 mm

AREA

9. Find the area of these shapes in cm².

a

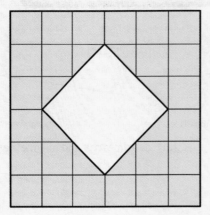

b

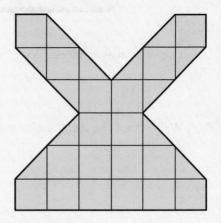

10. a   Draw a rectangle 6 cm long by 3 cm wide.

    b   Divide it into 1 cm squares, number the
        squares 1, 2, 3, ... and count to find the
        area of the rectangle.

    c   Now write down and use the formula to
        calculate its area.

1	2	3	...
...	...	...	

11. Calculate the area of each of these shapes :-

a

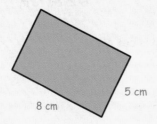

5 cm

8 cm

b

square

7 m

12. This rectangular sloping roof has to be covered in felt.

    a   Calculate the area of the roof in m².

    b   If the felt costs £4·00 per square metre,
        calculate the cost of felting the roof.

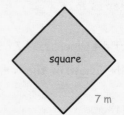

6 m

3·5 m

13.

3 cm

5 cm

a   Make an accurate drawing of this right angled triangle.

b   Draw a surrounding rectangle and calculate its area.

c   Now write down the area of the triangle.

14. Calculate the area of this right
    angled triangle in m².

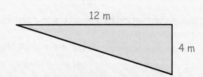

12 m

4 m

VOLUME

15. Put these shapes in order, starting with the one which has the **smallest** volume.

16. 3 lidfuls of plant food has to be given to a houseplant 3 times a week.

    The bottle holds enough plant food for 180 lidfuls.

    Will the plant food last the 18 weeks the plant is expected to bloom ? (*Explain*).

use lid →

17. A bottle holds 700 ml of liquid, a cup holds 200 ml and a teaspoon holds only 5 ml.

    a   I need 30 ml of food colouring for a cake mix. How many spoonfuls is this ?

    b   How many spoonfuls does the cup hold ?

    c   How many **full** cups does the bottle hold ?

    d   I bought 4 bottles of lemonade. How many cups can I fill ?

18. Write down the volume of liquid, (in millilitres),
    in this jar of strawberry concentrate.

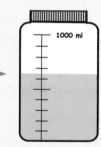

19. Write down the volume of each shape, in cm^3.

    a

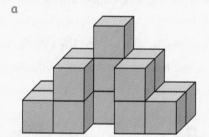

    b

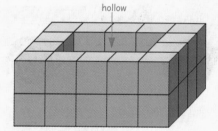

20. a   Change to millilitres :-   (i)   6 litres   (ii)   13·5 litres   (iii)   0·8 litres.

    b   Change to litres :-   (i)   4500 ml   (ii)   25 000 ml   (iii)   250 ml.

21. Find the volume of the concrete tower.

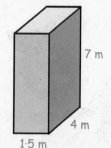

7 m

4 m

1·5 m

WEIGHT

22. List the following fruit in order, starting with the one that you think weighs least.

> apple - pineapple - plum - watermelon - grape.

23. Change from kilograms to grams :-

a   3 kg

b $\frac{1}{2}$ kg

c   16·5 kg

d   1 kg 200 g

e   5 kg 15 g

f $2\frac{3}{4}$ kg .

24. Change these weights to kilograms :-

a   3000 g

b   12 500 g

c   250 g

d   6400 g

e   5030 g

f   1005 g.

25.    Fiona and Beth weigh their suitcases before flying with Ryanjet.
Fiona's weighs $14\frac{1}{4}$ kg. Beth's suitcase weighs 13 kg 900 g.

How much more does Fiona's case weigh than Beth's (in grams) ?

26. An artist creates this structure out of blocks of concrete.

Calculate the total weight of the concrete structure.

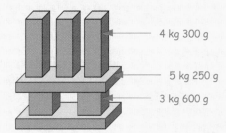

4 kg 300 g

5 kg 250 g

3 kg 600 g

27.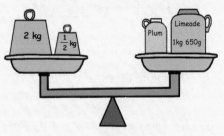

This truck is loaded with 6 identical, boxes.

The empty truck weighs 750 kg,

The loaded truck weighs 888 kg.

Calculate the weight of one box.

28. Two jars are placed on the scales.

The scales are perfectly balanced.

What is the weight of the Plum jar ?

29.

A fly (8 g) is eaten by a large spider (55 g) which is eaten by a mouse (250 g) which is eaten by a cat (2 kg 400 g) which is eaten by a fox ($12\frac{1}{2}$ kg).

How much does the fox now weigh ?

Consolidation of Patterns

1. Look at these three drawings. Draw the **4th** pattern in the sequence.

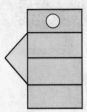 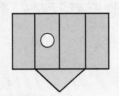 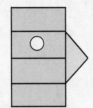   ....

2. a   Describe this pattern in words :-   8, 20, 32, 44, 56, ...

   b   Write down the next **four** terms of the pattern.

3. a   Here is another pattern. Describe this one :-   97, 88, 79, 70, 61, ...

   b   Write down the next **four** terms of this pattern.

4. Describe each of the following patterns and write down the next **four** terms each time :-

   a   8, 15, 22, 29, 36, ...   b   5, 23, 41, 59, ...

   c   83, 77, 71, 65, ...   d   1·8, 4·3, 6·8, 9·3, 11·8, ...

5. Write down the next **three** letters in these patterns :-

   a   A, D, G, J, ...   b   Z, X, V, T, R, ...

6. Here is a pattern made with tubs of pot noodles.

   a   Sketch the tubs for the 4th pattern.

   b   How many tubs do you need for a 4th pattern ?

   c   Copy the pattern 7, 14, 21 and then write down the next **five** terms.

   d   Make up a rule for this pattern. e.g. "Start at ..... and ......"

7. Write down :-

   a   the first **seven** square numbers   b   the 20th square number.

Chapter 14

Simple Linear Patterns

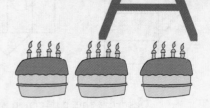

Be able to spot a pattern from a table and make up a simple rule for extending it

It is fairly easy to spot a number pattern from a diagram or a table.

Example :-

Each chocolate sponge has 4 candles.

Drawing up a table helps you see the pattern :-

No. of Sponges (S)	1	2	3	4	5	6
No. of Candles (C)	4	8	12	?	?	?

$\quad\quad\quad\quad\quad\quad\quad$ 4 $\quad$ 4 $\quad$ 4

Can you see that for every new sponge => the number of candles rises by 4 ?

=> $\quad$ We can write, in words :-

$$\boxed{\text{Number of Candles} = 4 \times \text{no. of Sponges}}$$

=> $\quad$ or in symbol form :- $\quad\boxed{C = 4 \times S}$

* For **12** sponges, you would need $C = 4 \times \textbf{12} = \textbf{48}$ candles.

Exercise 1

1. In a school library, the tables are set out so that 3 children sit around each table.

$\quad$ 1 table $\quad\quad\quad\quad\quad\quad$ 2 tables $\quad\quad\quad\quad\quad\quad\quad$ 3 tables
$\quad$ 3 children $\quad\quad\quad\quad\quad$ 6 children $\quad\quad\quad\quad\quad\quad$ 9 children

a $\quad$ Draw the next pattern of children sitting around 4 tables.

b $\quad$ Copy the following table and complete it :-

No. of Tables (T)	1	2	3	4	5	6
No. of Children (C)	3	6	9	?	?	?

$\quad\quad\quad\quad\quad\quad\quad\quad\quad\quad$? $\quad$? $\quad$?

c $\quad$ For every extra table, how many extra children are seated ?

d $\quad$ Copy and complete the formula :- **Number of children = ... × Number of tables.**

e   Now write down the formula using symbols :- C = ... × T.

f   Use your formula to decide how many children the library can take
     if there are 20 tables in it.

2.   Look at the star shapes with circles at each end point.

 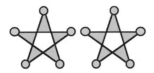 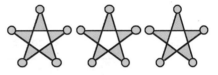

1 star   2 stars   3 stars
5 circles   10 circles   15 circles

a   Draw the next pattern of stars and circles.

b   Copy the following table and complete it :-

No. of Stars (S)	1	2	3	4	5	6
No. of Circles (C)	5	10	?	?	?	?

          ?   ?   ?

c   For every extra star, how many extra circles are needed ?

d   Copy and complete the formula :- **number of circles** = ... × **number of stars**.

e   Write down the formula using symbols :- C = ... × S.

f   Use your formula to decide how many circles are needed for 40 stars.

3.   Here is a glass of strawberry juice which needs 6 strawberries per glass to make it.

a   Copy and complete the table below listing the number of strawberries per 1 glass.

No. of Glasses (G)	1	2	3	4	5	6
No. of Strawberries (S)	6	?	?	?	?	?

          ?   ?   ?

b   How many strawberries are needed for 7 glasses ?

c   Copy and complete :- "the number of strawberries = ... × the number of glasses".

d   Write the formula using symbols connecting S and G.

e   Use your formula to say how many strawberries would be needed to make
     10 glasses of the juice.

4. Look at the price DJ Sports are charging for World Cup footballs :-

1 ball
£7

2 balls
£14

3 balls
£21

a   Copy and complete the table below showing the cost of buying the footballs.

No. of Footballs (F)	1	2	3	4	5	6
Cost in £'s (C)	7	?	?	?	?	?

? ? ?

b   Copy and complete :- Cost = ... x the number of footballs.

c   Write the formula using symbols connecting C and F.

d   Use your formula to find the cost to a football club wanting to buy 30 footballs.

5. Copy and complete this table which shows how many roses are expected to flower
on each rose bush in early spring.

No. of Bushes (B)	1	2	3	4	5	6
No. of Roses (R)	8	16	?	?	?	?

? ? ?

a   Copy and complete :- number of roses = ... x the number of bushes.

b   Write a formula using symbols connecting R and B.

c   Use your formula to find how many roses should flower from 50 rose bushes.

6. Copy and complete the following table which shows the number of marigolds in a pot.

No. of Pots (P)	1	2	3	4	5	6
No. of Marigolds (M)	10	20	30	?	?	?

a   Copy and complete :- number of marigolds = ... x the number of pots.

b   Write a formula using symbols connecting M and P.

c   Use your formula to find the total number of marigolds in 15 pots.

7. This table shows the number of small cherries there are to 1 large one on a cherry cake.

No. of Large Cherries (L)	1	2	3	4	5	6
No. of Small Cherries (S)	14	?	?	?	?	?

a   Copy and complete the table.

b   Write a formula connecting S and L and use it to find how many small cherries
there are to 20 large ones.

8. The table below indicates how many school minibuses, full of pupils, arrive at Belloch Academy each school day.

No. of Buses (B)	3	4	5	6	7	8
No. of Pupils (P)	60	80	100	?	?	?

a 3 school minibus can carry 60 pupils in total. How many pupils are allowed on one bus ?

b Write a formula connecting the number of pupils (P) and the number of buses (B).

c 18 minibuses, similar to those used by Belloch Academy, arrive at Ainsley High School each school day. Use your formula to calculate how many pupils in total are on these buses.

9. For each of the tables below, find a formula (or rule) connecting the two letters :-

a

No. of Newspapers (N)	1	2	3	4	5	6
No. of Pages (P)	30	60	90	?	?	?

$P = ? \times N$

b

No. of Trees (T)	1	2	3	4	5	6
No. of Pineapples (P)	18	36	54	?	?	?

$P = ? \times T$

c

No. of Days (D)	1	2	3	4	5	6
No. of Hours (H)	24	48	72	?	?	?

$H = ? \times D$

d

No. of Pounds (N)	2	3	4	5	6	7
No. of Pence (p)	200	300	400	?	?	?

$p = ? \times N$

e

No. of Muffins (M)	2	3	4	5	7	8
Cost in £'s (C)	2·50	3·75	5·00	?	?	?

$C = ? \times \ldots$

f

No. of Jars (J)	3	4	5	6	7	8
No. of Jelly Beans (B)	450	600	750	?	?	?

$\ldots = ? \times \ldots$

g

No. of Tubes (T)	2	4	6	8	10	12
Cost in £'s (C)	7	14	21	?	?	?

$\ldots = ? \times \ldots$

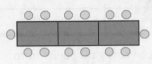

Look for a pattern in a table and make up a more complicated rule to extend it

Here is a pattern, showing children sitting around tables in their school dining area.

 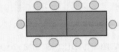

1 table	2 tables	3 tables
6 children	10 children	14 children

Drawing up a table will help you see a pattern.

No. of Tables (T)	1	2	3	4	5	6
No. of Children (C)	6	10	14	?	?	?

        4   4   4

For each additional table => the number of children rises by 4.

... but ..... No. of Children = 4 × no. of Tables or $C = 4 \times T$ doesn't work here !

Check :- $4 \times 1 \neq 6$, $4 \times 2 \neq 10$, $4 \times 3 \neq 14$, $4 \times 4 \neq 18$, $4 \times 5 \neq 22$

but $4 \times 1 + 2 = 8$ $4 \times 2 + 2 = 10$ $4 \times 3 + 2 = 14$ etc. does work

A correction number is required to make the pattern work. In this example, that number is 2.

=> $C = 4 \times T + 2$.

* With 10 tables, you can seat $C = 4 \times 10 + 2 =$ **42** children.

Exercise 2

1. Here is a pattern made with circles and squares.

 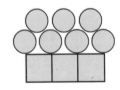

1 square	2 squares	3 squares
3 circles	5 circles	7 circles

  a   Draw the next pattern of circles and squares.

  b   Copy the following table and complete it :-

No. of Squares (S)	1	2	3	4	5	6
No. of Circles (C)	3	5	7	?	?	?

               ?   ?   ?

  c   For every extra square, how many extra circles are needed ?

cont'd.......

d   Write down the formula using **symbols** for calculating the number of circles needed if you know the number of squares.

$$C = ... \times S + ...$$

e   Use your formula to decide how many circles are needed with 10 squares.

2. In another school, the dining area tables are set out differently :-

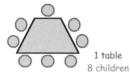
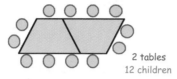
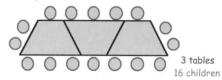

1 table
8 children

2 tables
12 children

3 tables
16 children

a   Draw the next pattern, showing children sitting around 4 tables.

b   Copy the following table and complete it :-

No. of Tables (T)	1	2	3	4	5	6
No. of Children (C)	8	12	16	?	?	?

         ?   ?   ?

c   For every extra table, how many extra children can be seated ?

d   Write down the formula using symbols :- $C = ... \times T + ...$

e   Use your formula to decide how many children can sit around 20 tables.

3. This table shows the cost of hiring a safety deposit box in a hotel :-

No. of Days Hired (D)	1	2	3	4	5	6
Cost in £'s (C)	8	11	14	17	20	23

         ?   ?   ?

a   How much will it cost to hire the safe for :-   (i) 4 days   (ii) 5 days ?

b   How much extra does it cost for each additional day of hire ?

c   Write down the formula for determining the cost of hiring the safe

$$C = ... \times D + ...$$

d   How much will it cost to hire the safe for 2 weeks ?

4. The weight of a truck carrying identical photocopying machines is given in the table.

No. of Photocopiers (P)	1	2	3	4
Total weight in kilograms (W)	1250	1300	1350	1400

a   How much does each extra photocopier weigh ?

b   What is the total weight of a truck carrying 5 photocopiers ?

c   Find a formula for the total weight $W = ... \times P + ...$

d   What is the total weight of a truck with 10 photocopiers ?

5.   Look at the pattern of fence posts and support panels.

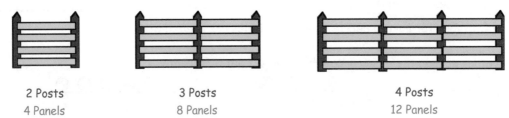

| 2 Posts | 3 Posts | 4 Posts |
| 4 Panels | 8 Panels | 12 Panels |

a   Draw the next pattern of fence posts and support panels.

b   Copy the table below and complete it :-

No. of Posts (*P*)	2	3	4	5	6	7
No. of Supports (*S*)	4	8	12	?	?	?

?   ?   ?

c   For every extra post, how many extra support panels are needed ?

d   Write down the formula using symbols   *S* = ... × *P* - ...

e   Use your formula to decide how many support panels
     are needed with 20 posts.

* note the correction number has
to be subtracted

6.   The designs below are made up of triangles and circles.

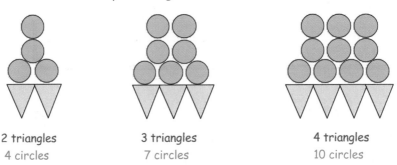

| 2 triangles | 3 triangles | 4 triangles |
| 4 circles | 7 circles | 10 circles |

a   Draw the next pattern of triangles and squares.

b   Copy the table below and complete it :-

No. of Triangles (*T*)	2	3	4	5	6	7
No. of Circles (*C*)	4	7	10	?	?	?

?   ?   ?

c   For every extra triangle, how many extra circles are needed ?

d   Write down the formula using symbols   *C* = ... × *T* - ...

e   Use your formula to work out how many circles sit on 50 triangles.

f   How many triangles are required if we have :-

     (i)   22 circles   (ii)   34 circles   (iii)   58 circles   (iv)   88 circles ?

7. Shown below are some tables connecting pairs of values.

Determine a **formula** or rule connecting the second letter in the table to the first letter.

a Tubs of apples lying on a wagon.

Tub (T)	1	2	3	4
Weight (W) kg	10	13	16	19

$$W = \dots \times T + \dots$$

b Fares for boat trips.

No. km (K)	1	2	3	4
Fare £'s (F)	2	7	12	17

$$F = \dots \times K - \dots$$

c Bees appear as flowers bloom.

No. Flowers (F)	1	2	3	4
No. Bees (B)	15	25	35	45

$$B = \dots \times F \dots \dots$$

d Time taken to grill chops on a barbecue.

No. Chops (C)	1	2	3	4
Grilling (G) min	7·5	8	8·5	9

$$G = \dots \times C \dots \dots$$

e Circles round triangles.

Triangles (T)	1	2	3	4
Circles (C)	12	16	20	24

$$C = \dots \times T \dots \dots$$

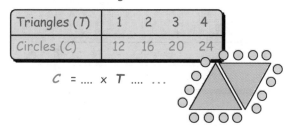

f Time taken to print pages.

No. Pages (P)	1	2	3	4
Time (T) seconds	30	36	42	48

$$T = \dots \times P \dots \dots$$

g Hiring a cement mixer.

Days hired (D)	1	2	3	4
Cost in £'s (C)	7	16	25	34

$$C = \dots \times D \dots \dots$$

h Filling a paddling pool using a hose.

Time mins (T)	1	2	3	4
Depth (D) cm	1·3	2·1	2·9	3·7

$$D = \dots \times T \dots \dots$$

i Weight of plant pot and daffodil bulbs.

No. of bulbs (B)	1	2	3	4
Weight (W) g	240	300	360	420

$$C = \dots \times I \dots \dots$$

j A stamp collection grows each year.

No. Years (Y)	1	2	3	4
No. Stamps (S)	100	350	600	850

$$S = \dots \times Y \dots \dots$$

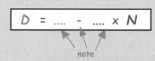

k The depth of water in a vase reduces as time goes on (evaporation).

$$D = \dots - \dots \times N$$

note

No. of days (N)	1	2	3	4
Water depth (D)	20	17	14	11

1. Draw the next picture in this pattern.

     . . . . .

2. Write down the next **three** numbers in each of these sequences :-

   a 4, 10, 16, 22, ..., ..., ...

   b 99, 87, 75, 63, ..., ..., ...

   c 1600, 800, 400, 200, ..., ..., ...

   d 7, 9, 12, 16, ..., ..., ...

3. Write down all the square numbers between 51 and 101.

4. Jenny's rate of pay is shown in the table below.

No. of Hours (H)	1	2	3	4	5
Wage in £'s (W)	8·20	16·40	24·60	?	?

   a What is Jenny's wage for :- (i) 4 hours   (ii) 5 hours ?

   b Write a formula connecting W and H using symbols.

   c Use your formula to find Jenny's wage for working 10 hours.

   d One week, Jenny's total pay was £246. How many hours had she worked ?

5. A girl is building a pattern with rectangular wooden building bricks.

  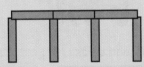 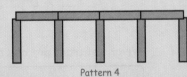

   Pattern 1   Pattern 2   Pattern 3   Pattern 4
   Bricks 3   Bricks ...   Bricks ...   Bricks ...

   a Draw pattern number 5 and count the number of bricks.

   b Copy and complete this table :-

Pattern no. (P)	1	2	3	4	5
Bricks needed (B)	3	...	...	...	...

   c Write a formula connecting B and P using symbols.

   d Use the formula to find how many bricks are needed for pattern 10.

   e What pattern number has 51 bricks ?

6. A joiner bills his customers with an initial call out charge plus an hourly rate.

   Examples of his charges are shown in the table :-

No. of Hours (H)	1	2	3	4	5	6
Charge in £'s (C)	42	52	62	?	?	?

   a   How much will it cost to call out the joiner for 4 hours ?

   b   How much extra does he charge for each additional hour ?

   c   Write down the formula for determining the cost of calling him out :-

$$C \;=\; \text{....} \times H \;+\; \text{....}$$

   d   What is his call out fee ?

   e   What does he charge for a job lasting 7 hours ?

   f   One job had to be done over 2 days, the total bill coming to £132.

   How many hours did this job take ?

7. The table below shows the price of junior golf clubs in a sale.
   You must buy more than 1 club to get the sale price.

No. of Golf Clubs (G)	2	3	4	5	6	7
Price in £'s (P)	19	29	39	?	?	?

   a   What's the price of 7 golf clubs ?

   b   How much extra is charged for each additional club ?

   c   Write down the formula for determining the cost of clubs :-

$$P \;=\; \text{....} \times G \;\text{....}\;\text{....}$$

   d   What is the price of 12 clubs ?

   e   Mr Montgomery paid £99 for clubs for his two daughters to share equally.

   How many clubs did each girl get ?

8. Shown below are two tables of values connecting pairs of letters.

   Write down a formula connecting the second letter to the first letter.

   a

P	1	2	3	4
M	50	55	60	65

   b

W	1	2	3	4
Z	9	13	17	21

Consolidation of Coordinates

1. a Which point has coordinates :-
   (i) (10, 3)   (ii) (8, 0)
   (iii) (3, 9)   (iv) (1, 10) ?

   b Write down the coordinates of :-
   (i) Q   (ii) U
   (iii) W   (iv) Z.

   c When 4 of the points are joined
      a parallelogram is formed.
      (i) Which 4 points ?
      (ii) Write down their coordinates.

   d Which point lies on the x-axis ?

   e Which point lies on the y-axis ?

   f Name the point which has its x-coordinate 1 larger than its y-coordinate.

   g Write the coordinates of the point which has its y-coordinate 1 larger
      than its x-coordinate.

   h Which 3 points have their x-coordinates the same as their y-coordinates ?

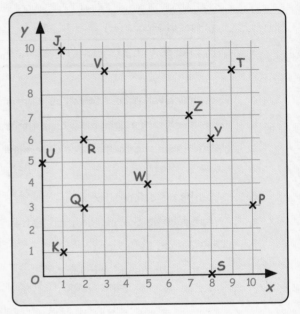

2. Draw a 10 by 10 coordinate grid as shown below.

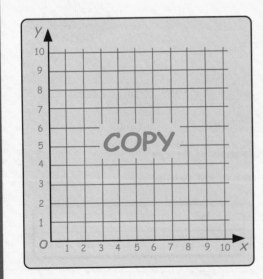

   a Plot the points A(3, 6), B(5, 2) and C(7, 6).

   b D is a point to be put on the grid so that
      figure ABCD is a kite with one diagonal
      measuring 6 boxes.

      On your diagram plot the point D
      and write down its coordinates.

   c Join A to C and join B to D.

      You now have both diagonals of this kite.

      Put a cross where the two diagonals
      meet, call the point K and write down
      its coordinates.

Chapter 15

Coordinates in 4 Quadrants   *Extension*

Be able to work with coordinates with positive and negative values

You should already know what a Coordinate (or Cartesian) Diagram looks like.

The *x*-axis is horizontal.

The *y*-axis is vertical.

O is the Origin.

M is the point 1 right and 3 up from the origin.

It has *x* coordinate 1 and *y* coordinate 3.   M(1,3).

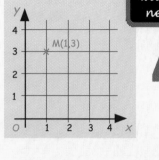

Both axes can also be extended backwards and downwards.

Look at the numbers on the new *x*-axis and *y*-axis.

They now include negative values.

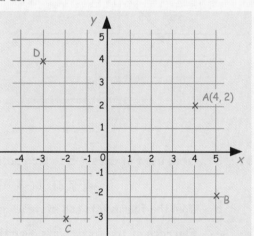

A is 4 right and 2 up from the origin.   A(4,2)

B is 5 right and 2 down from the origin.   B(5,-2)

C is 2 <u>left</u> and 3 down from the origin.   C(-2,-3)

D is 3 <u>left</u> and 4 up from the origin.   D(-3,4)

Exercise 1

1.   The coordinates of E in this diagram are E(-2, 3)

     Write down the coordinates of the other 8 points.

2.   Draw a large set of axes (-10 to 10 on both scales).

     Plot each set of points, join them up and say
     what shape is formed :-

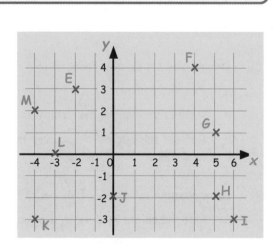

a   A(3,2) B(5,-3) C(3,-4) D(1,-3) A(3,2).

b   E(-4,4) F(-2,-7) G(-6,-7) E(-4,4) .

c   H(-3,7) I(3,5) J(3,-4) K(-3,-2) H(-3,7).

d   L(-5,1) M(-4,-4) N(1,-5) O(0,0) L(-5,1).

e   P(-10,2) Q(-8,3) R(-6,2) S(-6,-1) T(-8,-2) U(-10,-1) P(-10,2).

f   V(-3,-3) W(1,-3) X(3,-5) Y(-1,-9) Z(-5,-5) V(-3,-3).

3. a   Copy this diagram and plot
        the two points A(1,4) and B(4,–2).

    b   Find a 3rd point, (call it C),
        such that ABC is an isosceles triangle.

        Show C on your diagram,
        and write down its coordinates.

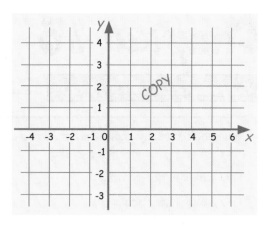

4.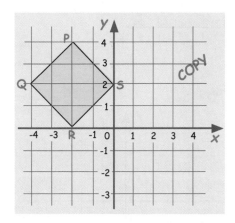

    a   Write down the coordinates of the 4 points,
        P, Q, R and S of square PQRS.

    b   Copy the diagram and flip PQRS over
        the x-axis.

        Write down the new coordinates
        of the corners of the square.

    c   Now flip your new square across
        the y-axis and write down the
        coordinates of the 3rd square.

5. a   Draw a set of axes, (–5 to 5 on both scales) and plot the four points

                K(–2,2), L(–3,–1), M(3,–1), N(4,2).

    b   Join the four points and state what type of shape is formed.

    c   Flip each of the four points over the x-axis to form a new four-sided shape.
        (This is called **reflecting** the shape).

    d   Write down the coordinates of the four corners of this new reflected shape.

6. Draw a new set of axes from –8 to 8 on both scales.

    a   Plot the 5 points E(6,1), F(7,4), G(2,6), H(–3,4) and I(–2,1). Join them up.

    b   Reflect your shape over the y-axis and write down the coordinates of your new shape.

    c   Reflect the **original** shape over the x-axis and write down the coordinates of your
        new shape.

7. Draw another set of axes from –6 to 6 on both scales.

    a   Plot the points T(–3,4), U(–1,6) and V(6,–1) and join T to U to V.

    b   Plot and write the coordinates of a fourth point, call it W, so that TUVW is a rectangle.

    c   Reflect TUVW in the y-axis and write down the coordinates of this new rectangle.

Revisit - Review - Revise

1. a   Which point has coordinates :-

   (i)   (7, 1)   (ii)   (0, –5)   (iii)   (–3, –4)   (iv)   (–4, 2) ?

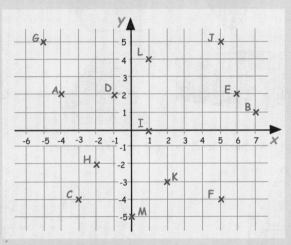

   b   Write down the coordinates of :-

   (i)   E   (ii)   F   (iii)   G   (iv)   H.

   c   When E and 3 other points are joined a kite is formed.

   (i)   Which 3 points ?   (ii)   Write down their coordinates.

   d   Which point lies :-   (i)   on the x-axis ?   (ii)   on the y-axis ?

   e   Name any 2 points   (i)   with the same x-coordinate

                                    (ii)   the same y-coordinate.

   f   Which 2 points have their x-coordinates the same as their y-coordinates ?

2.   Draw up a coordinate grid like the grid in question 1.

   a   Plot the points A(1, 4), B(–4, 1) and C(1, –2).

   b   D is a point to be put on the grid so that figure ABCD is a rhombus (diamond).

        On your diagram plot the point D and write down its coordinates.

   c   Join A to C and join B to D.

        You now have the two diagonals of the rhombus.

        Write down the coordinates of the point where the two diagonals meet.

   d   Reflect rhombus ABCD in the x–axis and write down the coordinates of the
        corners (vertices) of your new rhombus.

Consolidation of 3 Dimensions

1. What 3-dimensional mathematical shape is each of the following :-

   a   b   c   d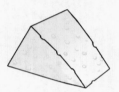

   e   f   g    h

2. State what 3-D shapes have been used to make up these figures :-

   a 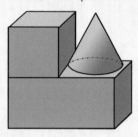   b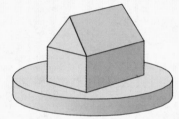

3. How many :-

   a   edges does a cuboid have

   b   faces does a cylinder have

   c   vertices does a cube have

   d   edges does a triangular prism have

   e   faces does a square based pyramid have

   f   vertices does a hemisphere have

   g   edges does a cone have

   h   faces does a triangular prism have

   i   vertices does a cone have

   j   faces does a sphere have ?

4. Which 3-dimensional figure would you get if you cut out each shape and folded it ?

   a 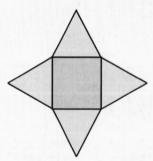   b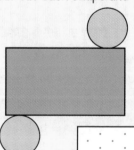

5. Use isometric (dotty) paper to draw a cube with sides measuring 4 boxes.

   Dotty paper needed

Chapter 16

Nets of Cubes

Be able to recognise
and draw
Nets of Cubes

What is meant by "Net" ?

The net of a Cube is the shape you obtain when the solid shape,
made of e.g. cardboard, is "opened up and laid it out flat".

- A cube consists of 6 faces.
- All 6 faces are congruent (the same).
- Each face is a square.

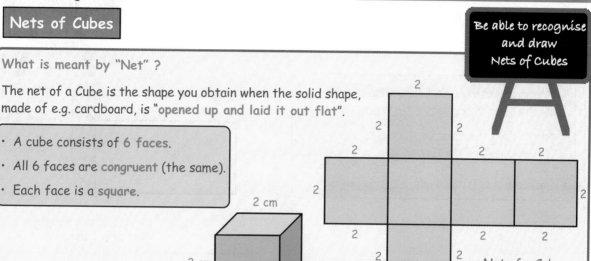

2 cm

Net of a Cube

Exercise 1

You will need squared paper and a ruler for this exercise.

1. Draw a full size net for a cube with sides 3 centimetres.

2. Draw a net of a cube with sides 1·5 centimetres.

3 cm

3. Shown below are shapes made up of 6 congruent squares.
   For each one, decide if it is the **net** of a cube or not. (Drawing/tracing and cutting out may help).

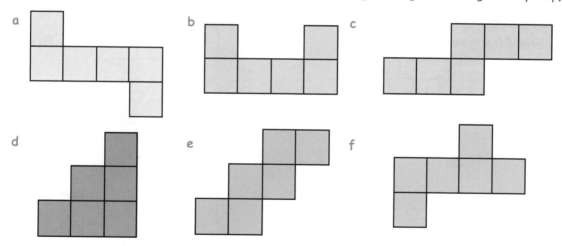

a   b   c

d   e   f

4. Design a further two nets of a cube, different from any of those found in question 3.

5. Let us look at a special family of nets of cubes. Each starts with four squares in a row.

   a   Decide on a simple rule where to put the other 2 squares
       so that you will **always** get the net of a cube.

   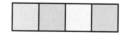

   b   Say where you would **not** put the 2 squares if you wanted a cube net.

The net of a Cuboid is the shape you obtain when the solid shape, made of e.g. cardboard, is "opened up and laid it out flat".

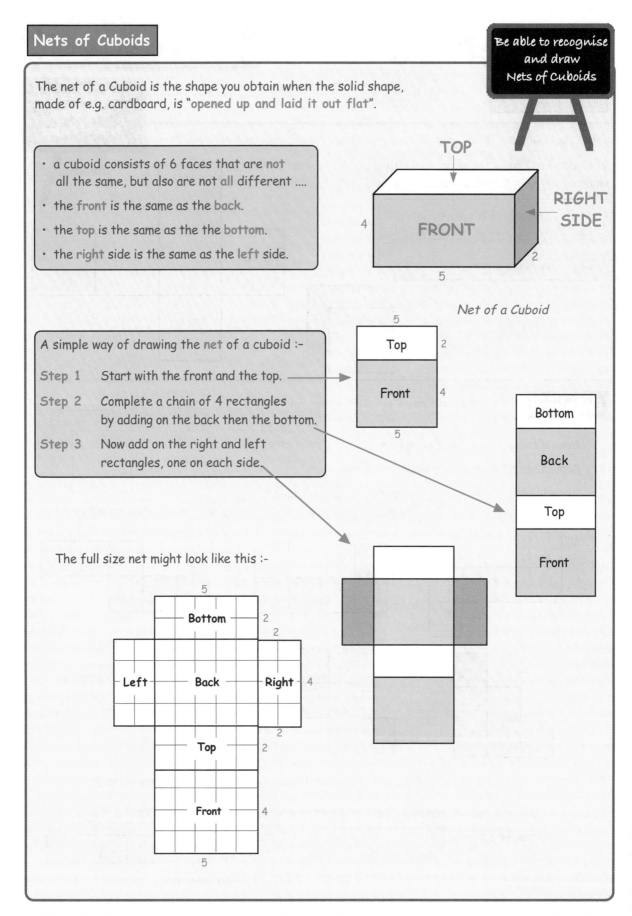

- a cuboid consists of 6 faces that are not all the same, but also are not all different ....
- the front is the same as the back.
- the top is the same as the the bottom.
- the right side is the same as the left side.

Net of a Cuboid

A simple way of drawing the net of a cuboid :-

Step 1   Start with the front and the top.

Step 2   Complete a chain of 4 rectangles by adding on the back then the bottom.

Step 3   Now add on the right and left rectangles, one on each side.

The full size net might look like this :-

You will need squared paper and a ruler for this exercise.

1. Here is part of a net of a cuboid measuring 8 by 2 by 3 (boxes).

    a   Copy this carefully onto squared paper and add the back and front.

    b   Now add the left and right faces.

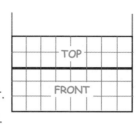

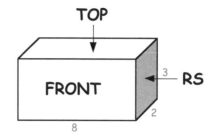

2. Part of the net of this cuboid is shown opposite.

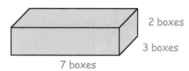

    2 boxes

    3 boxes

    7 boxes

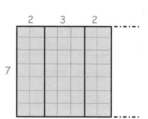

    a   Make a neat full size copy of this net.

    b   Complete the net showing all the faces.

3. Neatly, draw nets of the following cuboids :-

    a   b   c

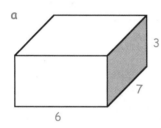

    3

    7

    6

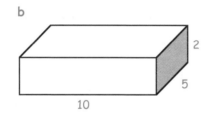

    2

    5

    10

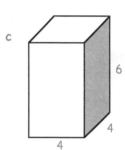

    6

    4

    4

4. Make sketches of the boxes corresponding to these nets and fill in their dimensions :-

    a   b   *note - units are cm, not boxes !

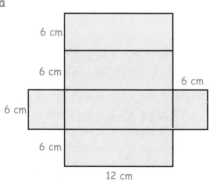

    6 cm

    6 cm

    6 cm

    6 cm

    6 cm

    12 cm

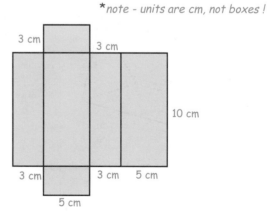

    3 cm

    3 cm

    10 cm

    3 cm   3 cm   5 cm

    5 cm

5. a   Draw a possible net of this cube and this cuboid on cardboard.

    b   Cut your nets out and fold them to form solid shapes.

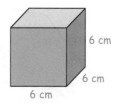

    6 cm

    6 cm

    6 cm

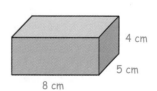

    4 cm

    5 cm

    8 cm

Nets of Triangular Prisms & Other Shapes

The Triangular Prism

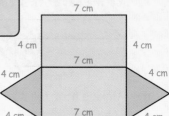

4 cm 4 cm 4 cm 7 cm

- The Triangular Prism shown has **5 faces**, but they are **not** all the same.
- The front is the same as the back. (Equilateral Triangles)
- The three "wrap-around" faces are the same. (Rectangles)

A simply way of drawing the net :-

Step 1   Start with a strip of 3 rectangles each 4 cm by 7 cm.

Step 2   Use compasses to draw the 2 equilateral triangles.

Net of a Triangular Prism

7 cm
4 cm   4 cm
7 cm
4 cm   4 cm
4 cm   7 cm   4 cm
4 cm   4 cm
7 cm

Exercise 3
You will need a ruler and a pair of compasses.

1. Draw a **full size** net of the triangular prism shown above.

2. Draw the net of the triangular prism shown opposite.
    (You might like to do it on card, cut it out and sellotape it together to make the prism.)

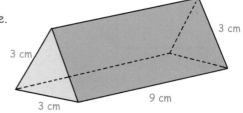

3 cm   3 cm   3 cm   9 cm

3.

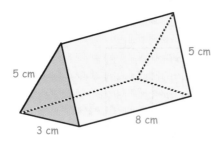

5 cm   5 cm   3 cm   8 cm

This triangular prism has its end faces in the shape of **isosceles** triangles.

a   Write down the dimensions (*the length and breadth*) of each of the three rectangular faces.

b   Make an accurate drawing of its net, using your ruler and pair of compasses.

4. A sketch of the net of this **right angled** triangular prism is shown beside it.

Make an accurate drawing of the net.

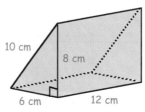

10 cm   8 cm   6 cm   12 cm

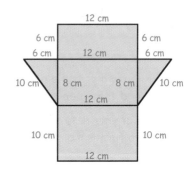

12 cm
6 cm   6 cm
6 cm   12 cm   6 cm
10 cm   8 cm   8 cm   10 cm
12 cm
10 cm   10 cm
12 cm

---

5. a Name each of these 3-dimensional shapes.

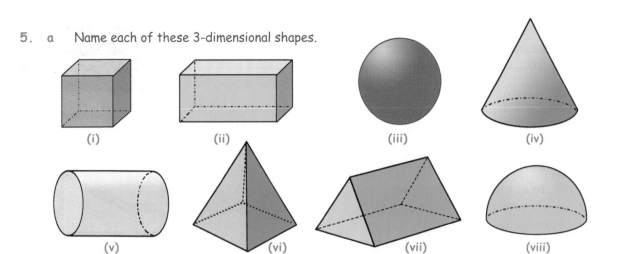

(i)   (ii)   (iii)   (iv)

(v)   (vi)   (vii)   (viii)

b Which 3-D figures do you get when you cut out the following shapes and fold them up ?

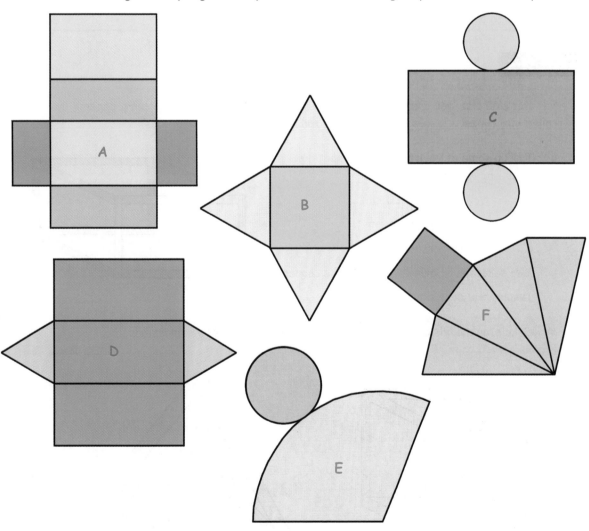

6. Calculate the total surface area (3 rectangles + 2 triangles) of the triangular prism in Q4.

Skeletons of Solids - Some Practical Work

The skeleton of a 3-D Shape consists of the "bones" of the shape.

It is the "wire frame" that shows the outline of a shape.

Can you see that, to make the skeleton of this cuboid, we would need 12 straws ?

skeleton of a cuboid

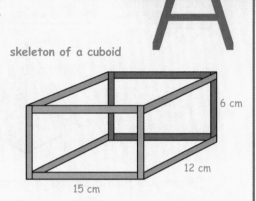

Four pieces measuring 15 cm.
Four pieces measuring 12 cm.
Four pieces measuring 6 cm.

Total length of straw = (4 x 15) + (4 x 12) + (4 x 6)

= 60 + 48 + 24

= 132 cm.

Exercise 4

For this exercise, you are going to need straws or lots of pieces of A4 plain paper rolled into tubes, scissors and sellotape. (*You may wish to work in groups*).

1. a Roll up some of your paper, sellotape them and cut them so you have :–

   • four pieces of 20 cm

   • four pieces of 15 cm

   • four pieces each 10 cm.

   b Use sellotape or blue tack to join the corners.

   Display the best skeleton .

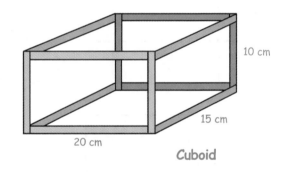

Cuboid

2. Make skeleton models of each of the following shapes as neatly as possible.
   (*You may wish to work in groups – see your teacher*).

a

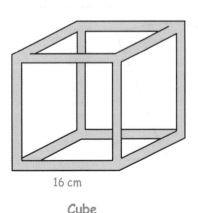

16 cm

Cube

b

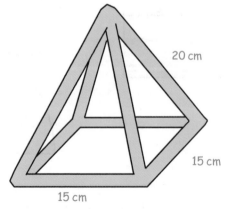

20 cm

15 cm

15 cm

Square Based Pyramid

2. c

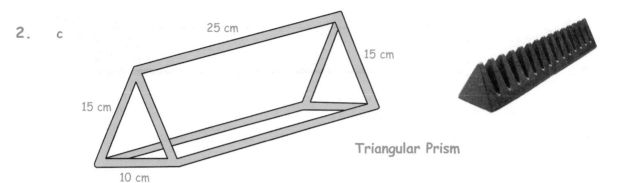

25 cm

15 cm

15 cm

10 cm

Triangular Prism

3. a Look at your cube in Question **2a**. What is the **total** length of straw needed to make this cube ?

b What is the **total** length of straw needed to make the square based pyramid in Question **2b** ?

c What is the **total** length of straw needed to make the triangular prism in Question **2c** ?

4. a Use your straws to make this model house.

b What is the total length of straw needed to make it ?

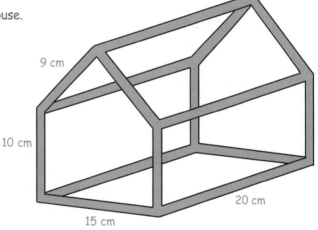

9 cm

10 cm

20 cm

15 cm

5. Make a model of this tower.

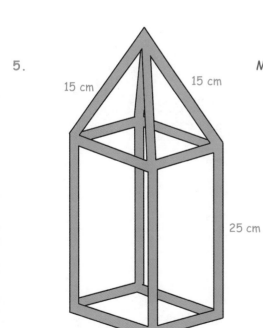

15 cm

15 cm

25 cm

12 cm   12 cm

1. Name the 2-dimensional and the 3-dimensional mathematical shapes shown below :-

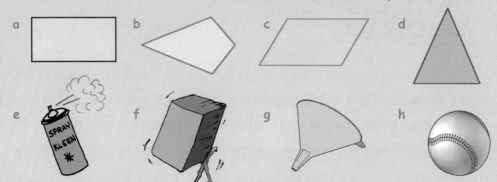

    a   b   c   d

    e   f   g   h

2. How many sides has :-

    a   a hexagon   b   an octagon   c   a decagon ?

3. Make a sketch of each shape below and indicate which sides/angles are equal.

    State also how many lines of symmetry it has.

    a   square   b   rhombus   c   parallelogram.

4. Copy and complete the table to show the number of edges, faces and vertices which some 3-dimensional shapes have.

3-D Shape	No. Edges	No. Faces	No. Vertices
cube		6	
cuboid			
cone			
cylinder			
$\triangle$ prism			
Sq. pyramid			5

5. What 3-D shape is made up of :-

    a   6 squares   b   3 rectangles and 2 triangles

    c   4 triangles and 1 square   d   2 circles and 1 rectangle ?

6. Which well known 2-D quadrilateral shape am I describing ?

    a   I have 4 equal sides but my end angles are not right angles.

    b   I have only 1 axis of symmetry.

    c   My opposite sides are equal and parallel, but I don't have any axes of symmetry.

    d   I have 4 lines of symmetry.

7. List 3 statements that are true about the 3-D shape, "hemisphere".

8. Write down the 3-D shape that each net below could make :-

a 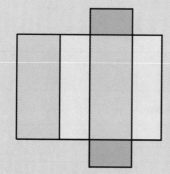   b 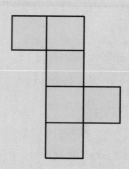   c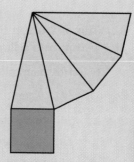

9. Make a neat sketch of a net for each of these 3-D shapes :-

a 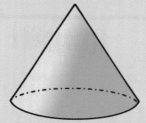   b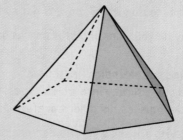

10. Make an accurate drawing of the net of these shapes :-

a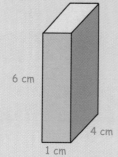

6 cm

4 cm

1 cm

b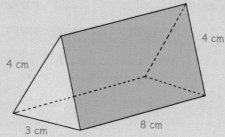

4 cm

4 cm

3 cm   8 cm

11. On squared paper, make a neat sketch of a :-

   a   square   b   rectangle   c   rhombus

   d   kite   e   parallelogram   f   equilateral triangle.

12. On plain paper, make a neat sketch of a :-

   a   cube   b   cuboid   c   cone

   d   cylinder   e   square based pyramid f   right angled triangular prism.

13. On square dotty paper AND triangular dotty paper, make sketches of :-

   a   cubes   b   cuboids

   c   triangular prisms d   square based pyramids.

Consolidation of Statistics

1. This pictograph shows the number of people waiting at a railway station one morning.

   Key:  stands for 25 people.

   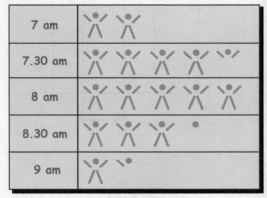

7 am	
7.30 am	
8 am	
8.30 am	
9 am	

   a How many people were at the station at :-

      (i) 7 am   (ii) 7.30 am

      (iii) 8.30 am   (iv) 9 am ?

   b How many more people were there at 8 am than 7 am ?

   c Suggest a reason why 8 am was the busiest time at the station.

   d Give a reason why 7 am was not so busy .

   e Why do you think the station was quieter at 9 am ?

2. The owner of an Indian Restaurant carried out a survey into which types of chicken dishes his diners preferred.

   The results are shown in the bar graph.

   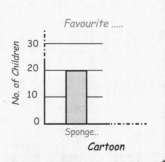

   Favourite Food

   a How many diners chose :-

      (i) salsa   (ii) tikka

      (iii) jalfrezi   (iv) jaipuri ?

   b What dish was liked by the fewest and how many chose it ?

   c 100 diners chose the all time favourite dish, chicken curry. It is not shown in the graph.

   Why would it be difficult to show this statistic ? Explain !

3. A survey was carried out at Blairgowrie Nursery School as to which cartoons the children enjoy. The results are shown below.

SpongeBob	Tom & Jerry	Bugs Bunny	Scooby Doo	Mickey Mouse	Yogi Bear
60	70	75	90	10	15

   Use the given scale to draw a bar chart illustrating them.

   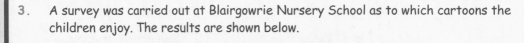

4. In a survey carried out outside Gordon's the Bakers last Saturday, people were asked to name their favourite pastry.

donuts	buns	eclairs	apple pie	muffins
buns	eclairs	muffins	donuts	donuts
donuts	buns	buns	buns	donuts
buns	muffins	donuts	buns	apple pie
buns	donuts	buns	muffins	eclairs
donuts	buns	apple pie	buns	muffins

a   Draw a frequency table to show this information with the use of tally marks.

b   Draw and label a neat bar graph to represent this information.

5. The diagram below shows the numbers of birthday cakes sold in Gordon's the Bakers the following week.

a   How many cakes were sold on Tuesday ?

b   On which two days were the same number of cakes sold ?

c   How many more birthday cakes were sold on Friday than on Wednesday ?

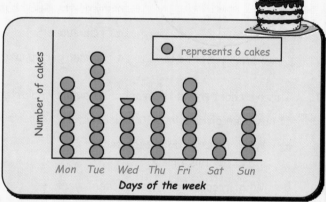

6.

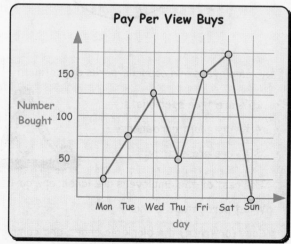

This line graph shows the number of pay per view films bought from a TV company during one week.

a   How many films were bought on :-

   (i) Wednesday   (ii) Friday ?

b   Which is the most popular day to buy films ?

c   How many more films were bought on a Friday than on a Tuesday ?

d   Between which 2 days was there the largest rise in film sales ?

e   Give a possible reason for the Sunday figure that week.

7. The driving range "Golf World" of Milngavie kept a record of the number of golf balls they rented out (in thousands) over a nine month period.

Month	Mar	Apr	May	Jun	Jul	Aug	Sep	Oct	Nov
No. Balls (1000)	4	7	12	20	18	22	15	8	1

a   Draw a neat labelled line graph to show the renting figures.

b   Why are the numbers for March, April, October and November lower than the others ?

8.

Fried Supper Sales

A survey of fried supper sales from a fish & chip van was made and the results are shown on the pie chart.

The pie chart is divided into **8** sectors.

Each sector is one eighth of the whole pie.

If the survey represented 400 people, how many of the 400 chose :–

a   fish supper

b   sausage supper

c   hamburger supper

d   pudding supper ?

9.   This pie chart shows the number of pupils who attended the school christmas dance.

It has been divided into **20** equal sectors.

a   What fraction does each sector stand for this time ?

b   What fraction of those present were :–

(i)   boys   (ii)   girls ?

c   There were 200 pupils at the dance.

How many of them were :–

(i)   boys   (ii)   girls ?

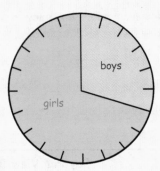

Pupils at the dance

10.

COPY

Of the employees in a councils' parks department :–

· 15% are tree specialists

· 45% are plant gardeners

· 30% are grass cutters

a   The rest of the employees are landscape gardeners.

What percentage is that ?

b   Copy (or trace) the blank pie chart, and complete it showing the above information.

11. Shown are the prices for 2 different airlines flying first-class from London to Dubai.

	April	May	June	July
Ryanjet	£690	£855	£982	£1160
Fly Dubai	£700	£850	£990	£1140

a How much will it cost to travel to Dubai with Fly Dubai in May ?

b If you want the cheaper flight in July - which airline should you choose ?

c Talisa Sarwar travelled to Dubai from London for £982.

 (i) Which airline did she fly with ? (ii) In which month did she travel ?

12. Here is a part of a calendar for the month of February 2011.

Sun	Mon	Tues	Wed	Thur	Fri	Sat
		1	2	3	4	5
6	7	8	9	10	11	12
13	14	15	16	17	18	19
20	21	22	23	24	25	26
27	28					

a On what day of the week was February 14th (Valentine's day) ?

b On what day of the week was the last day in February ?

c (i) What was the date 2 weeks after February 8th ?

 (ii) What day was it ?

d (i) What was the date 13 days before February 12th ?

 (ii) What day was it ?

e It was February the 18th. My anniversary was in two weeks time.

 On what day and what date was my anniversary ?

f Three weeks before February the 7th I bought a piano.

 On what day and date was that ?

g What day of the week was March 6th ?

h On what day was All Fool's Day, April 1st ?

13. State three things that are wrong with this graph, which was produced by Lodl to show how their prices compare with the other two supermarkets for a certain brand of goods.

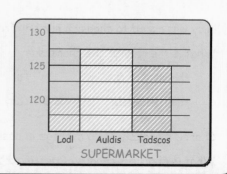

Chapter 18

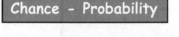
Chance - Probability

Understand Chance (Probability) and predict the likelihood of a simple event happening

What is meant by "Probability" ?

When we talk about the probability of an event happening, we mean the chance or likelihood of the event taking place.

Example :-   What is the probability or chance that everyone in the class likes the same flavour of ice cream ?

Do you think this is possible, impossible or certain ?

Predict the outcome, and then ask other people in your class what they think about ice cream in a survey.

Were your thoughts close to what you found ?

Exercise 1

Use these words to answer the following questions :-

(certain - likely - an even chance - unlikely - impossible)

1. Willis places cards numbered 1-8 face down on the table.

    If he picks one card at random how likely is it that :-

    a   he will choose the card with 3 on it

    b   he will choose a card with a number from 1 to 6 on it

    c   he will choose a card marked 15 ?

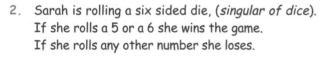

2. Sarah is rolling a six sided die, (*singular of dice*).
    If she rolls a 5 or a 6 she wins the game.
    If she rolls any other number she loses.

    Should she have more wins or losses ?

3. Lucy was asked to choose a number from 1 to 10.

    What is the chance she chooses :-

    a   the number 5   b   an even number

    c   the number 12   d   any number from 2 to 9 ?

4. Charlie's goal shooting average in basketball is 80 out of 100.

    What is Charlie's chance of getting a basket the next time he shoots ?

Probability

The **probability** of something happening is often written as :-

the number of times that it can happen, in relation to the total number of possible outcomes.

Example :-   A die is marked 1 to 6.

If you choose a number from the die then roll it, there is an **equal** chance of rolling each number.

We say there is a **one in six** chance of rolling your number.

We also say the **probability** of rolling your number is 1 in 6 or $P(6) = 1$ in 6.

Exercise 2

1.   Sarah tosses a £2 coin in the air.

What is the **probability** that it will land showing a tail ?

2.

Willis is playing the game Rock, Scissors, Paper.

What is the **probability** that he will choose Rock on his next turn ? (i.e. what is **P(Rock)** ?)

3.   Ben finds that he doesn't know whether to go left or right at the corner when he is going to the hospital.

What is the **probability** that he is correct if he **guesses** the way ?

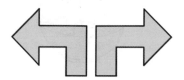

4.   In a group of boys, 4 are right handed and 1 is left-handed.

What is the **probability** of correctly guessing which child is left-handed ?

5.   There are 8 fish in a bowl. One is silver and the rest are gold.

What is the **probability** of the silver fish being fastest ?

6.

There are 3 pink marbles and 1 blue marble in a jar.

What is the **probability** that on your first pick you will choose the blue marble ? (i.e. what is **P(blue)** ?)

Simplifying Probabilities

Miss Lee's pencil case contains **10 green biros** and **2 red biros**.

She takes one out without looking to see what colour it is.

The probability that she will take a **green biro** is 10 out of 12.

We can simplify this to 5 out of 6   (we divide both numbers by 2).

The probability that she will take a red biro is 2 out of 12.

We can simplify this to 1 out of 6   (divide both numbers by 2).

Always simplify a probability if it is possible to do so.

Example :-   A probability of 6 out of 15 simplifies to 2 out of 5.

7.  In a paddock there are 12 sheep. Six are brown and six are white.

What is the **chance** that a white sheep will come out first when the gate is opened ?

8. The names of each of the 6 **states** and the 3 **mainland territories** of Australia are written on separate pieces of paper and placed in a hat.

James pulls a piece of paper out of the hat. What is the **probability** he will choose one with a **state** written on it ?

9.  A fruit bowl contains 4 apples, 6 oranges and 2 bananas.

If Jenna asks her mum to pass her a piece of fruit, what is the **probability** she will be handed :-

a   an apple   b   an orange

c   a banana   d   a pear ?

10. Dave is asked to write down what month he was born.

What is the **probability** he was born in a month beginning with the letter J ? (P(J)).

11.  In a horse race there are 8 runners with equal ability. The first and second horses past the post win a prize.

What is the **chance** for **each** horse to win a prize ?

12. A boy tosses two coins at the same time.

What is the **probability** that they both show heads ?

13. Two dice are thrown and the 2 numbers showing are added together.

What is the **probability** that the total of the two dice comes to :-

a   2   b   9   c   less than 5   d   13 ?

The 3 Я's

Revisit - Review - Revise

1. Write a list of 3 things that might happen at school or at home next week.

   Use the words :- certain, likely, even chance, unlikely, impossible.

2. A hospital has records showing that boys and girls are born in equal numbers.

   What is the chance that the next new baby born will be a boy ?

3. 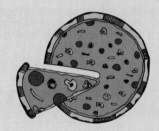 In a box of ice lollies there are 5 orange and 1 green ice lolly.

   What is the probability of taking out the green one if you can't see inside the box ?

4. What is the probability of rolling a :-

   a   4 on a six-sided die

   b   1 or a 2 on a six-sided die ?

5. Tom has 3 coins in his pocket totalling £2.05. If he takes out one coin from his pocket, what is the probability that it is a 5 pence coin ?

6. There are 7 classes in a school.

   The head teacher decides to select one class each week to have a pizza party.

   In the first week, what is the probability that Lucy's class is the one chosen to have the party ?

7. In a pack of cards there are 26 red and 26 black cards.

   What is the probability of choosing a red card ? (P(red).

8. There are 9 children in a race. They are all fast runners.

   What is the probability for each child to be in the first 3 ?

9. 4 girls and 8 boys write their names on a piece of paper and put them in a hat.

   What is the probability that the first time :-

   a   a girl's name will be pulled out   b   a boy's name will be pulled out ?

Chapter 19

Revision

Revise all the work covered in CfE Level 2

Do NOT use a calculator except where you see the  sign.

1. Round to the nearest 1000 :-   a   12 098   b   35 501.

2. Copy and complete :- The answer to 4728 + 1876 is about 4700 + ... which equals ....

3. Write the number that comes :-   a   300 after 9900   b   500 before 17 200.

4. Write in words :-   a   20 806   b   3 207 080.

5. Find the following :-

    a   2680
      + 530

    b   22 708 + 9550   c   12 000
                          − 1836

    d   16 300 − 8762.

6. Find the following :-

    a   2617
       × 6

    b   12 070 × 9   c   5 ⟌ 7165   d   90 336 ÷ 8.

7.   a   Eight identical wooden blocks weigh 3576 grams. What is the weight of 1 block ?

    b   A bottle holds 750 ml of juice. How much juice is there in half a dozen bottles ?

    c   Alex earns £2355 per month and Jane earns £1987. How much do they earn altogether ?

    d   I have flown 1695 km of my 3070 km journey. How much further have I still to travel ?

8. To what numbers do these arrows point ?

    a 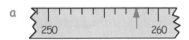   b    c

9. Write down the answers to the following :-

    a   5017 × 1000   b   330 800 ÷ 100   c   321 × 300   d   6 400 000 ÷ 4000.

10. What number must have gone INTO this number machine ?

11. Round :-

    a   29·663 to the nearest whole number   b   12·109 to 1 decimal place

    c   5·097 to 2 decimal places   d   199·96 to 1 decimal place.

12. Do the following :-

    a   19·8 + 2·77   b   121·83 − 35·9   c   8·07 × 6   d   31·27 ÷ 2

    e   55 + 6·7 + 0·69   f   31 − 8·76   g   19·75 ÷ 5   h   13·16 × 8.

13. Find :-

    a   6·0301 x 10   b   236 ÷ 1000   c   0·234 x 1000   d   6·8 ÷ 100.

14. Find :-

    a   10 – 2 x 3   b   3 + 7 x 5   c   20 ÷ (4 + 6)   d   28 + 12 ÷ 4 - 7.

15. What is the temperature on this thermometer ?

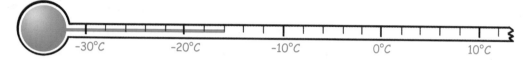

16. Find :-

    a   5 – 11   b   –2 + 8   c   6 + (–10)   d   (–21) – 9.

17. Write down the next two numbers in these patterns :-

    a   16, 20, 24, 28, ...   b   81, 74, 67, 60, ...   c   9, 7, 5, 3, ...   d   1, 2, 4, 8, ...

18. Write down the first ten multiples of   a   3   b   13.

19. Write down all the factors of   a   12   b   50.

20. Write down all the prime numbers less than 50.

21. What fraction of this triangle is coloured red ?

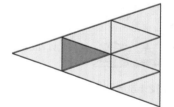

22. What fraction of these dominoes contain a six ?

23. What percentage of this circular lattice has been coloured yellow ?

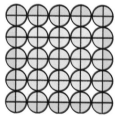

24. At a birthday party, 25% present were men, 35% were women, 30% were girls and the rest were boys.

    What percentage were boys ?

25. Write down any fraction equivalent to   a $\frac{3}{5}$ b $\frac{7}{11}$.

26. Simplify as far as possible :-   a $\frac{21}{28}$ b $\frac{12}{18}$.

27. What is :-   a $\frac{2}{3}$ of £2·40   b $\frac{3}{7}$ of 350 metres ?

28. Rewrite these numbers in order, puting the smallest first :-   0·45, $\frac{2}{5}$, 35%.

29. Express as a fraction, simplifying it as far as possible.   a   55%   b   24%.

30. Find :-   a   10% of £80·00   b   25% of £1·60   c   50% of 65p.

31. 16 out of 20 people said their dog ate Cham dog food. What percentage is this ?

32. I picked up 2 shirts at £9·50 each, a top at £17·50 and a tie costing £6·75.

    I checked my wallet and discovered a £20 note, two £10 notes and two £5 notes.

    Will I then have enough left over for my £1·50 train fare home ? (*Explain your answer*).

33. Which of these chocolate bars gives the better deal ? (*Explain your answer showing working*).

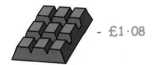 - £1·08    - £1·10

34. I changed £200 into dollars when the rate was £1 = $1·60.

    How many dollars did I receive ?   £1 = $1·60

35.    A butcher bought 8 kilograms of frying steak for £37·50.

    He sold the steak to his customers at £6·50 per kilogram.

    How much profit did he make altogether ?

36. Write in 12 hour form, using am or pm :-   a   1550   b   0010.

37. Change :-   a   125 seconds into mins and secs.   b   5 hours 25 mins to mins.

38. Find :-   a   2 mins 35 secs + 5 mins 45 secs   b   5 mins 20 secs – 1 min 55 secs.

39. The stopwatches show the times for the winner
    and the runner up in an 800 metre race.

    Who won and by how much ?

Owens   Davis

40. On the 11th December 2011, the sun rose at 8.33 am and set at 3.44 pm.

    How long was it between sunrise and sunset ?

41. a   A car travelled the 560 kilometres from Glasgow to London. It took exactly 8 hours.
        Calculate the car's average speed.

    b   I walked in the countryside for 4 hours. My average walking speed was 6 km/hr.
        How far did I manage to walk ?

    c   I cycled the 60 kilometres from my house to the coast. My average speed was 20 km/hr.
        How long did it take me ?

42. Estimate the height of the classroom door in centimetres.

43. Estimate the area of this shape in cm².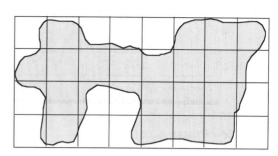

44. Measure the lengths of these lines and express your the answer to each in 3 different ways.

a

b

45. Change to centimetres :-   a   5 metres 36 cm   b   10 m 4 cm.

46. Change to kilograms :-   a   2 kg 345 g   b   5 kg 50 g.

47. How many millilitres are in :-   a   3 litres 200 ml   b $4\frac{3}{4}$ litres ?

48. It is $4\frac{1}{2}$ kilometres to the cinema. I walked 850 metres to the bus stop where I caught the bus. How far is it from the bus stop to the cinema ?

49. Write down the areas of these two shapes :-

a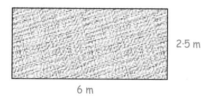
2·5 m
6 m

b
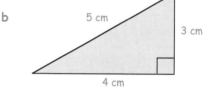
5 cm
3 cm
4 cm

50. The perimeter of this shape is 60 cm.

Calculate the length of the smallest side.

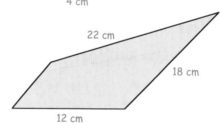
22 cm
18 cm
12 cm

51.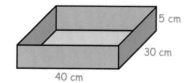
5 cm
30 cm
40 cm

a   Calculate the volume of this container in cm³.

b   How many litres will the container hold when full ?

52. This table shows the connection between the number of hexagonal shaped tables in a school dining room and the number of metal legs.

Number of hexagonal tables (H)	1	2	3	4	5
Number of legs (L)	6	12	18	24	30

Find the formula connecting L and H.

L = ...

53. This table shows the combined weight (*W*) in kg of a wooden tray loaded with various numbers (*N*) of metal cubes. Find the **formula** connecting them.

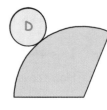

Number of cubes (N)	1	2	3	4	5
Total weight (W) kg	8	11	14	17	20

W = ... x ... + ...

54. **Solve** these equations for *x* :-

    a $x + 5 = 12$ b $3x = 24$ c $2x - 1 = 9.$

55. Write down all the solutions for $p > -2$ from this set of possibilities :-   {-3, -2, -1, 0, 1, 2, 3}.

56. Write down three ways in which a rectangle and a parallelogram are **different** .

57. How many **edges** has a square based pyramid ?

58. Which solid 3-D shapes are made up from these nets ?

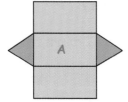
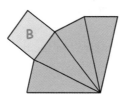
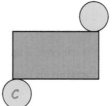

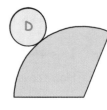

59. What **type** of angles are shown ?   a   b

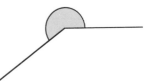

60. **Measure** these angles and write down their sizes :-

    a   b

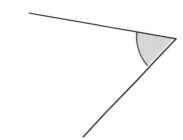

61. On a compass, what direction is directly opposite **South East** ?

62. **Measure** and write down the **3 figure** bearing of Brassaw from Aisley.

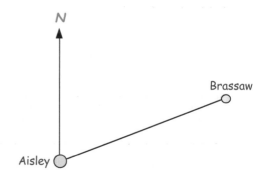

63.

7 cm

This spear has been drawn to a scale of 1 cm = 12 cm.

What is the length of the **real** spear ?

64. a   Write down the **coordinates** of point **A**.

b   Write down the **coordinates** of a 4th point,
(call it **B**), so that **ABCD** is a rhombus.

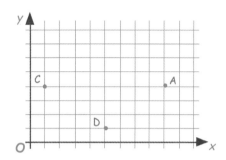

65.

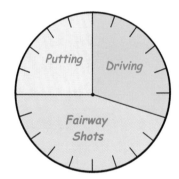

This piechart has 20 sectors.
It shows what a group of men thought their best golf shots were.

What **percentage** of the men felt "driving" was the
strongest part of their game ?

300 men from the golf club took part in this survey.
How many of them believed driving was their strongest ?

66. A 12 sided die numbered 1 to 12 is rolled. A game is won if a **multiple** of 3 shows.

What is the **probability** of winning the game ?

67. If the probability it will rain today is $\frac{7}{10}$, what is the **probability** it will **NOT** rain today ?

68. **Copy** both shapes and **complete** so that the dotted line is a **line of symmetry** each time.

a

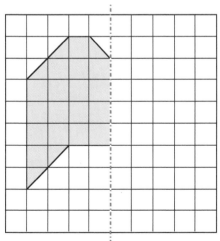

b

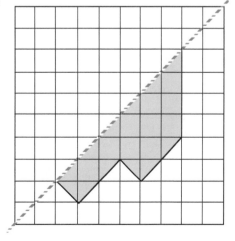

answers to Book 2b

Consolidation of Whole Numbers

1. a twenty thousand and sixty
    b seven hundred and two thousand and five
2. a 20830 b 65004
3. 28889, 28982, 29028, 29208, 30002, 30010
4. a A = 360, B = 520, C = 4250, D = 4380
    b 56°
5. a 3000 b 71000
6. a 91 b 306 c 7700 d 64
    e 1620 f 2700 g 22399 h 8987
7. £1·04
8. a 6901 b 3684 c 7383 d 4518
9. a 70 b 580 c 4000
10. a 1200 b 7000 c 56900
11. a 170 b 600 c 9000 d 10000
12. a 318 b 57519 c 4856 d 10715
13. a 56 b 1783 c 1387 d 539
14. a 470 b 23100 c 50400 d 60000
    e 970 f 800 g 490 h 16
15. a 5243 b 1458 c £417
    d 753 l e 2515 kg
16. a 5684 b 54
18. For whole numbers simply add on 6 zeros

Chapter 1 - Exercise 1 (page 3)

1. a 1 million b 7 thousand
    c eighty thousand
    d 400 thousand e ninety
2. a 7 hundred b seventy
    c 7 thousand e 7 million
3. a four thousand and eighty
    b twenty one thousand nine hundred
    c seventy one thousand three hundred and fifty
    d two hundred and thirty five thousand and eighty
    e seven hundred and three thousand four hundred and sixty
    f 1 million eight hundred and seventy thousand
    g four million ninety three thousand and seventy
    h twenty seven million fifty thousand and sixty two
4. a 4209 b 17050 c 60098 d 230001
    e 5407000 f 1000007
    g 12060040
5. a 6786-6867-6876-7008-7068-7080-7086
    b 90887-98999-99924-100076-100086-100870
6. a 330 b 2190 c 394140 d 10850
    e 273001 f 598500 g 983700 h 3100000

7. A 480 B 7900 C 9100 D 1660
    E 1840 F 1500 G 2200 H 13900
    I 14700 J 30000 K 45000 L 125000
    M 250000 N 650000 O 780000 P 25500
    Q 26800 R 28300 S 200000 T 460000
    U 720000
8. a 975 b 3450 c 44350
    d 850000 e 780500 f 1070000
9. a 1000000 b 500000
    c 250000 d 750000
10. a £161653000
    b One hundred and sixty one million, six hundred and fifty three thousand
11. Four million four hundred thousand
12. a 14000000000 b various

Chapter 1 - Exercise 2 (page 5)

1. a 340 b 1260 c 1140
    d 1650 e 8920 f 14280
    g 12200 h 13600 i 69000
    j 169600 k 48000 l 1170000
2. a 13080 b 24680 c 10450
    d 193080 e 68600 f 98480
    g 585630 h 65520 i 274140
    j 246900
3. a 43200 b 105600 c 228000
    d 125300 e 151600 f 183000
    g 292500 h 325600 i 738900
    j 1464000 k 4236000 l 1808000
    m 2202000 n 952000 o 14301000
    p 47880000
4. a 1200 b 7200 c 28000
    d 45000 e 350000 f 48000
    g 180000 h 450000 i 2100000
    j 5400000 k 28000000 l 48000000
5. a 70 b 70 c 700
    d 60 e 60 f 3000
    g 7000 h 51000 i 7000
    j 520 k 3100 l 630
6. a 760000 miles b 125
    c £1390 d 72000
7. a 192 b 2893 c 5 888 896

Chapter 1 - Exercise 3 (page 7)

1. a 60 b 40 c 70 d 40
    e 20 f 180 g 380 h 290
    i 10 j 410 k 590 l 330
    m 2770 n 9800 o 7100
2. a 300 b 900 c 800 d 800
    e 300 f 800 g 4700 h 4100
    i 9500 j 7200 k 26300 l 29900
    m 16100 n 7900 o 20500

3. a 9000 b 23000 c 49000
    d 38000 e 57000 f 92000
    g 20000 h 77000 i 84000
    j 74000 k 17000 l 358000
    m 436000 n 369000 o 800000
4. a 489950 b 489900 c 490000
5. a £24360000 b £24000000
    c £20000000

Chapter 1 - Exercise 4 (page 8)

1 62 × 78 = 60 × 80 =4800 - close to 4836
2 a 2379 b 3204 c 34998
   d 33988 e 536
3 a 2100 b 2000 c 7200
   d 24000 e 24000 f 160000
   g 40 h 100 i 30
   j 200 k 100 l 50
4 a 16000 grams b £500
   c 8000000 miles

Chapter 1 - Exercise 5 (page 9)

1 £2800
2 £465000
3 £1085744
4 a 53000 b 1484000
5 a 37223 b 20331
6 10080
7 315
8 £1137
9 a £540 b £58
10 525000
11 64
12 12
13 No she overspends by £80
14 18
15 2354
16 425
17 a £20160 b £19885
18 £5175000
19 a Jenny 1.45 Brother 1.48
   b Brother

Chapter 1 - Exercise 6 (page 11)

1 a 24 b 17 c 12 d 16
   e 55 f 7
2 a 0 b 1 c 0 d 2
   e 15 f 12 g 20 h 18
   i 10
3 a 11 b 2 c 45 d 10
   e 30 f 33
4 a 35 b 5 c 54 d 34
   e 26 f 44 g 50 h 2
   i 14
5 a (5+3)×2=16 b 18 -(5×2)+8
   c (20+4)÷6=4 d 10+(6÷2)×5=25
   e 10+20÷(5-1)=15 f 5+2×(8-6)÷2=7

Consolidation of Symmetry (page 14)

1. If you can fold a shape over a line and the two halves fit exactly then the line is a line of symmetry.

2. a 2   b 1   c 0   d 1
   e 12   f 5   g 3   d 0

3. a   b   c
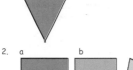

4. a   b   c
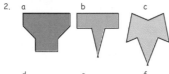

Chapter 2 - Exercise 1 (page 15)

1.
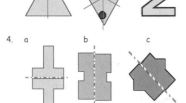

2. a   b   c
   d   e   f
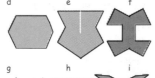

g   h   i

3. a   b   c
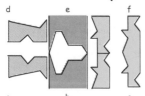

d   e   f

4. a   b   c
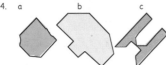

---

d   e   f

g   h   i

j   k   l

5. a   b   c

d   e   f

g   h   i

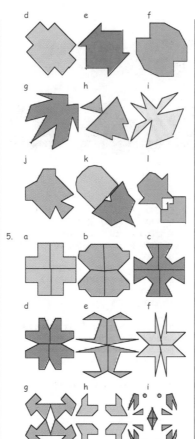

6. various
7. various
8. See Fonts

Consolidation of Time (page 20)

1. a 3.02 am   b 6.40 pm
   c 10.38 am   d 11.45 pm
2. a 0530 b 1702 c 2340 d 1200
   e 0045 f 2155 g 0010 h 1945
3. 7 hr 50 mins
4. 12.15 pm
5. a 1055 b 35 min c 25 mins d 1720
6. a (i) 30 (ii) 31 b 16 days
7. a Kate by 24 minutes
   b May - 4 hr 24 mins, Kate - 3 hr 36 mins
8. 1745

Chapter 3 - Exercise 1 (page 21)

1. a 0830 b 2050 c 1300 d 2000
   e 0100 f 2125
   g 0320 Sat   h 0205 Wed
   i 0340 Tue   j 0410 Sun
2. a 8.50 am   b 11.32 am
   c 12.30 pm   d 11.25 pm
   e 6.00 pm   f 2.00 am Tue
   g 3.50 pm   h 12.30 am Fri
   i 5.10 am Sat   j 6.10 am Thu
3. a 2230   b 7.32 pm
   c 0110   d 1555
   e 3.10 am   f 2300 Sat
   g 10.40 pm Mon   h 10.30 pm Tue
   i 2.15 am Tuesday   j 5.30 pm Fri

---

4. a 6 hr   b 2 hr 30 min
   c 2 hr 35 min   d 3 hr 55 min
   e 7 hr 50 min   f 11 hr 10 min
   g 4 hr 50 min   h 4 hr 30 min
   i 3 hr 45 min   j 36 hrs
5. 11 hrs 35 min
6. No. Was 3 minutes late
7. Yes. With 5 minutes spare
8. 2.12 am
9. a 10 hr 10 mins   b 2105 Mon
10. a 2 days 10 mins
    b 3 days 5 mins
    c 1 day 2 hr 40 mins

Chapter 3 - Exercise 2 (page 23)

1. a 12.57 am   b 12.32 am
   c 5.32 pm and 3.53 am
   d 2 minutes   e 11 mins
   f 11 mins   g 3 hr 57 mins
   h 4 hr 23 mins   i 9 hrs 59 mins
   j Just - by 6 mins
   k the 2115 London to Perth train
2. a The holiday is to Orlando Florida on
      Monday at 10.05 am for 14 days and the
      flight number is TAX328. The holiday is
      available between the 27th June and the
      18th July.
   b Naples for 7 or 14 days.
   c at 4.30 am with Direct Breaks
   d The holiday is to Majorca Spain on
      Saturday at 9.45 pm for 10 days and the
      flight number is DBX1139. The holiday is
      available only on the 15th October.
   e Sunday at 1.15 pm with Direct Breaks
   f Naples with Flight number FCX1544
   g (i) Same date
      (ii) different time, number of days,
           Flight number and Company
   h Number of days and Company
   i The holiday is to Malaga Spain on
      Sunday at 1.15 pm for 7 days and the
      flight number is DBX4534. The holiday is
      available from the 8th May to the 16th
      October.
3. Project

Chapter 3 - Exercise 3 (page 25)

1. 2 mins 35 seconds
2. a 1 min 20 secs   b 2 mins 18 secs
   c 3 mins 30 secs   d 5 mins
   e 15 mins 30 secs   f 10 mins
3. a 1 hr 35 mins   b 2 hrs 15 mins
   c 4 hrs 15 mins   d 8 hrs
   e 20 hrs 10 mins   f 100 hrs
4. a 8 mins 55 secs   b 9 mins 20 secs
   c 12 hrs 20 mins   d 3 mins 15 secs
   e 5 mins 15 secs   f 40 mins
5. 10 mins 35 secs
6. 1 day 1 hr and 30 mins
7. a 2 592 000 seconds
   b 315 360 000 approx not taking into
      account leap years. If you take it there
      are 365 and a quarter days in a year it
      is 315 576 000 seconds

Chapter 3 - Exercise 4 (page 26)

1. a (i) 33 (ii) 3 min 15 sec (iii) 8 min 8 sec
   b (i) 1 min 24 secs (ii) 3 mins 7 secs
      (iii) 8 mins 30 secs
   c (i) 1 hr 13 mins (ii) 2 hrs 25 mins
      (iii) 5 hrs 48 mins
   d (i) 6 min 15 secs (ii) 9 hrs 30 mins

(iii) 2 mins 50 secs

2. a 3·9 secs   b 5·0 secs
  c 12·6 secs   d 18·6 secs
  e 24·2 secs   f 8·0 secs
  g 5·4 secs   h 19·8 secs
  i 0·4 secs

3. McGovern, Goodwin, Samson, Van Zanten, Thomson, Murray

4. 2 mins 54·61 secs

5. 2 mins 55·14 secs. USA won by 0·53 secs.

6. 0·25 of a second

7. 14 mins 27·42 secs

8. a 1 min 23·02 secs b 4 mins 16·25 secs
  c 7 mins 6·08 secs d 3 mins 0·04 secs
  e 58·93 secs

9. a 4 hrs 13 mins 25·08 secs
  b 8 hrs 49 mins 10·84 secs
  c 11 hrs 59 mins 0·02 secs

10. 1 min 13·2 secs

11. a Pete   b 3·06 seconds

12. a 2·08 secs   b 3 mins 2 secs

13. a Selleck   b 2·72 secs
  c 3 mins 43·41 secs

14. a 4 mins 13·1 secs b 6 hrs 53 mins

15. Can't be done without re-crossing 1 bridge

Answers to CHAPTER 4 (Page 31)

Consolidation of Decimals (page 31)

1. a 0·7   b 2·3   c 3·8
2. a 0·6   b 2·3
3. a 0·25   b 4·24   c 0·07
4. a hundredths   b thousandths
5. a units b hundredths   c tenths
  d hundreds   e thousandths
6. a 1·008, 1·098, 1·8, 1·898, 1·97, 2·001, 2·090
  b 0·807, 0·89, 0·908, 0·967, 0·976, 0·977, 1·102
7. a 4 units + $^7/_{10}$ + $^3/_{100}$ + $^8/_{1000}$
  b 7 units + $^2/_{10}$ + $^8/_{100}$ + $^5/_{1000}$
  c $^4/_{10}$ + $^1/_{100}$ + $^6/_{1000}$
  d 2 tens + $^5/_{10}$ + $^2/_{1000}$
  e $^1/_{100}$ + $^3/_{1000}$
8. a 8·7   b 8·12   c 0·58
  d 2·189 e 3·69 f 7·9
9. a 29·8   b 5·5   c 5·67
  d 22·36 e 67·53 f 7·05
  g 0·8   h 0·36 i 0·46
10. a A=11·5 B=12·4 c=13·8
  D=14·4 E=15·5 F=16·3
11. a £8   b £2   c £19   d £19
  e £12   f £1   g £1   h £188
12. a 7 cm b 9 cm c 3 cm d 12 cm
  e 13 cm f 70 cm g 41 cm h 100 cm
13. a 1   b 5   c 8   d 36
  e 16   f 27   g 15   h 342
14. a 8·2   b 2·9   c 11·5   d 18·5
  e 4·0   f 14·9   g 0·3   h 0·1
15. a 5·3   b 305·9 c 23·2
  d 17·4 e 3·6   f 25·2
16. a 0·4   b 0·3   c 1·8   d 0·6
17. a 11·8   b 55·9   c 6·4
  d 5·4   e 31·4   f 7·5
18. 9·37   b 3·85   c 13·27 d 19·51
  e 4·01   f 23·90 g 0·28 h 0·10
19. a 1·8 m   b 1·9 kg
20. a 4·9   b 30·9   c 42·3   d 12·23
  e 0·808 f 1·266 g 1·534 h 21·416
  i 40·76 j 21·558 k 787·99 l 338·358
  m 0·3   n 3·4   o 38·1   p 2·07

  q 12·78 r 206·54 s 2·916 f 1010·139
21. a 14 cm b 3·68 m c 54·1 cm
22. a 16·32 kg   b 2·87 km
  c (i) £39·45 (ii) £15·55
  d Drew 3·3 km, Tara 3·78 km Tara 0·48 km
  e Ally 34·88 m, Chere 34·68 m Chere 20 cm
23. a 95·2   b 999·11 c 1036·8 d 4871·4
24. a 61·6   b 110   c 198·575 d 24077·04
25. a 25·6 kg   b £269·36
  c 1408 g   d Alex - £2·35 more
26. a 12·69 b 15·83 c 15·94 d 5·64
27. a 3·8   b 8·9   c 4·03   d 29·07
28. a 48·2 kg   b £19·33 c 14·63 km
29. a 86   b 18   c 10·1   d 0·2
  e 323·87 f 51·01 g 0·07 h 0·102
30. a 532   b 944   c 203   d 550
  e 1112·3 f 15·5 g 1·76 h 0·94
31. a 1147 b 6060 c 1340 d 56100
  e 789   f 65·4 g 1010·1 h 700·7
32. a 44lb   b 440 lb c 4400 lb
33. a 8435 b 91700 c 100   d 1
34. a 4·31   b 8·88   c 2·305 d 1·5
  e 0·9   f 0·054 g 0·06   h 0·0011
35. a 1·595 b 7·5332 c 0·451 d 0·8704
  e 8·8   f 0·95 g 0·011 h 0·005
36. a 3·5982 b 325·876 c 4·56 d 0·8341
  e 0·12 f 0·4   g 0·0343 h 0·011
37. a 1·21 g f £17·58 c £33200
38. a 2·6   b 19·0   c 0·8
  d 9·17 e 0·08 f 99·77 g 0·01
39. a 9·91 b 3·7   c 135·6 d 1·15
  e 34·8 f 0·089 g 2583 h 19·76
  i 176·4 j 1910 k 234·61 l 123·227
  m 356·28 n 0·16 o 0·04 p 100
40. a 1·03 m b 26·96cm c 12·5 m
  d 15·6 kg e 5·13 m
41. a 14   b 2   c 8
  d 6   e 16   f 55
  g 0   h 1   i 0
  j 2   k 15   l 12
  m 6   n 2   o 45

Chapter 4 - Exercise 1 (page 38)

1. a 6   b 100, 8 c 1000, 9 d 10, 7
2. a 26·4 b 3663·9 c 2246·8 d 652·4
3. a 529·2 b 847·2 c 355·59
  d 21880 e 4626 f 171710 g 943·2
  h 60·8 i 146   j 54850 k 70·2

Chapter 4 - Exercise 2 (page 39)

1. a 9   b 100, 7 c 1000, 5
2. a 4·23 b 0·412
3. a 1·61   b 3·47   c 1·039 d 10·94
  e 0·0191 f 0·3505 g 0·1002 h 0·026
  i 0·0442 j 0·024 k 0·000161 l 0·142
4. a 0·68   b 485·6 c 0·649 d 0·109
  e 0·0285 f 16800 g 0·038 h 0·016
  i 1239 j 0·0033 k 0·02   l 495
5. Check all answers

Answers to CHAPTER 5 (Page 41)

Consolidation of Decimals (page 41)

1. a obtuse b acute c straight
  d right   e reflex f obtuse
2. a 53°, 2°, 39°, 63° b 127°, 178°, 126°, 97
  c 90°   d 180°   e 184°, 300°
3. a ∠PEC b ∠UNT c ∠BOA
4. a 30°   b 157°
5. See diagrams
6. a 90°   b 135° c 225° d 315°

Chapter 5 - Exercise 1 (page 43)

1. See drawings
2. See drawings
3 a/b/c   See drawings
4. a/b/c/d/e See drawings

Chapter 5 - Exercise 2 (page 45)

1. See drawings
2. See drawings
3 a/b/c   See drawings
4. a/b/c/d See drawings

Chapter 5 - Exercise 3 (page 47)

1. See drawings
2. See drawings
3 a/b/c   See drawings
5. Cannot be done because the length of WG is bigger than the combined lengths of the two smaller sides GR and WR.

Chapter 5 - Exercise 4 (page 48)

1. a 20°   b 15°   c 65°   d 47°
  e 150° f 130° g 55° h 145°
2. a 110° b 130° c 195° d 35°

Answers to CHAPTER 6 (Page 51)

Consolidation of Compass Points (page 51)

1.

2. a 90°   b 180° c 225°
  d 225° e 315° f 135°
3. a SE   b N   c SE
  d (i) 135° (ii) 315°
4. a/b/c   See drawings

Chapter 6 - Exercise 1 (page 52)

1. a 7 cm, 3·5 cm   b 42 m, 21 m
2. a 2 cm   b 3 m   c 9m
3. a 120 cm b 240 cm c USA
4. a 8.10 m b 4·05 m
5. a 5 cm   b 15 m
6. a 6 cm by 4·5 cm b 240 m by 180 m
  c 840 m
7. a 6·5 cm b 1·95 m c 1·05 m
8. a 16 cm b 1·92 m
9. a 320 m by 240 m b 1120 m
10. a 5 cm b 50 km c (i) 62 km
  c (ii) 66 km   d 52 km
11. a 6·3 cm b 126 miles
  c (i) 96 miles (ii) 150 miles (iii) 98 miles
  d 410-420 miles
12. 2·2 - 2·3 km

Chapter 6 - Exercise 2 (page 55)

1. Rectangle measuring 6 cm by 4 cm
2. Rectangle measuring 12 cm by 7 cm
3. Rectangle measuring 3 cm by 8 cm
4. Rectangle measuring 5 cm by 12 cm
5. a Triangle 8 cm long by 5 cm high
  b 6·4 cm ----> 1280 m long
6. Isosceles triangle 6 cm tall by 15 cm long

7.

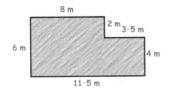

8.

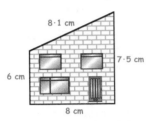

9. a Triangle 11 cm long and 9 cm high
    c About 140 metres

Chapter 6 - Exercise 3 (page 58)

1. a See drawing   b 4·4 cm c 13·2 m
2. a See drawing   b 15·5 cm c 155 m
3. a (i) See drawing (ii) 10·6 m
    b (i) See drawing (ii) 250 m
    c (i) See drawing (ii) 92 m
    d (i) See drawing (ii) 1300 m
4. a See drawing   b 4·95 m
5. a See drawing   b 45 m
6. a See drawing   b 11·5 km c 25·3 km
7. About 31 km

Chapter 6 - Exercise 4 (page 60)

1. a 180°   b 135°   c 045°   d 270°
    e 090°   f 225°   g 315°   h 000°
2. a SE   b W   c NW   d N
    e S   f NE   g SW   h E
3. a 010°   b 085°   c 150°
    d 255°   e 187°   f 300°
4. a 310°   b 195°   c 352°
5. a/b

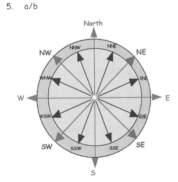

    c 000°, 022·5°, 045°, 067·5°, 090°, etc

Chapter 6 - Exercise 5 (page 62)

1. a 050°   b 150°   c 090°   d 165°
    e 025°   f 005°   g 065°   h 100°
2. a 035°   b 060°   c 110°   d 085°
    e 155°   f 125°   g 095°   h 020°
3. a 315°   b 260°   c 205°   d 290°
4. a 250°   b 300°   c 200°   340°
5. See drawings

Consolidation of Money (page 65)

1. a £5·25 b £5 note + 20p and 5p coins
2. a £30·60 b £21·89 c £32·34 d £4·16
3. Pack of 4 - 14p each, Pack of 6 - 13p √
4. 300 ml - 94p/100ml, 500 ml - 90p/100ml √
5. a £19·75 b £79·00
6. a £73·70   b £62·50

Chapter 7 - Exercise 1 (page 66)

1. a Scotia b Ms Ann E String
    c end of Apr 2011 to end of Aug 2014
2. a Card no. 2311323458980041
       Mrs Ruth Wilson Feb 2013 to Jan 2015
       Sort code 200347 Account 00176502
    b Card no. 18174000389880032
       Mr Alex Dunbeath Dec 2012 to Nov 2016
       Sort code 314502 Account 00453198
3. a To identify the bank branch
    b To differentiate between customers
    c In case you lose your card or it is stolen
    d Faster and safer at times
4. Various
5. Discussion

Chapter 7 - Exercise 2 (page 67)

1. £4·80 + £160 = £164·80
2. £14·40 + £480 = £494·40
3. a 2%
    b (i) £795·60 (ii) £1836 (iii) £352·41
4. a £82 b £902 c £2193·50
5. Vira is cheapest (33%)
6. a Discussion   b discuss

Chapter 7 - Exercise 3 (page 68)

1. a No - £570 - £25 short   b 1 week
2. 2 more weeks
3. a A - 8 weeks, T - 7 weeks √   b 1 week
4. a 13 weeks   b 1 weeks
5. a £40 + 5 × £5 = £65 £5 over budget
    b Budget for £65 or diet more

Chapter 7 - Exercise 4 (page 69)

1. £90
2. £12·50
3. £22300
4. £6500
5. £331 - £315 = profit of £16
6. Profit of £430
7. £5400
8. £2495
9. £118
10. £12·50
11. £62
12. a £87   b £17
13. 85p
14. a 20   b £12   c £5·50
15. a 15   b £172·50 c   £22·50
16. £5 each

Chapter 7 - Exercise 5 (page 71)

1. a £55 b £120 c £155
    d £1800 e £140 f £6·75
2. a £123 b £155 c £144 d £57
3. a £57 b £150

Chapter 7 - Exercise 6 (page 72)

1. + £780 = £830   b £830 c £80
2. £250 + £1890 = £2140   b £340

3. a £1069·50   b £119·50
4. a £5203   b £553
5. a £345   b £50
6. a £13600   b £1100
7. a £365 b same
    c To encourage people to buy from them
8. a £1200 b £200 per month
9. a £570   b £57
10. a £0   b £23
11. £708·50 - £650 = £58·50
12. a £900 + £4350 = £5250   b £750
13. CheapJeep £3580
    Jeeps-R-Us £3630
    JeepCo   £3175 best buy
14. £100 per month

Chapter 7 - Exercise 7 (page 75)

1. €276
2. €575
3. a €115 b €414   c €943
    d €3220 e €28·75 f €10·98
4. a €26·45 b €138   c €15·64
    d €253 e €552   f €1667·50
5. a $510   b 96000 Yen
    c 1875 HK dollars d 24000 pesos
6. a $2400
7. a $425 b €287·50 c 17500 d 300
8. Same price £250 = 400 Australian dollars
9. a Cheaper in Scotland - €287·50
    b Cheaper in USA - Britain $2750
    c Cheaper in Italy - Britain €16675
10. Various
11. Various

Chapter 7 - Exercise 8 (page 77)

1. £300
2. £80
3. a £1478·26   b £273·91
    c £869·57   d £203·48
    e £26·09   f £51·74
4. £369·57
5. a £4·00   b £10·00
    c £3·20   d £413·04
    e £126·09   f £69565·22
6. £10·00 (12 francs)
7. America - £5·82   Australia - £6·50
    India - £4·27   France - £5·91
    Hong Kong - £5·12 Cheapest in India
8. £418
9. Not quite - about £1·09 short
10. €1·13 to the £1
11. 41·18 Rupees
12. a 6086·96 Rupees b 32869·57 Yen
    c €10·35   d $3120 Australian
    e 1117647·06 Dollars f $3187
13. Varies dependent of exchange rates
    a Kuna - Croatia
    b SEK - Sweden
    c Ruble - Russia
    d Baht - Thailand

Chapter 8 - Exercise 1 (page 81)

1. a 3°C   b -3°C   c -6°C   d -8·5°C
    e 18°C   f -4°C   g -15°C h -32°C
2. a -£50
    b (i)   balance of £72
       (ii) overdrawn by £55
       (iii) nothing in bank - owe nothing
       (iv) overdrawn by £225·75

c -£5 d -£14 e -£16 f -£105
g £27 h -£1·80 i £2250 j £192

Chapter 8 - Exercise 2 (page 83)

1. See drawing
2. a 19°C b 12°C c 21°C d 6°C
   e 10°C f 2°C g -10°C h 5°C
   i -7°C j -18°C k -19°C l -21°C
   m -3°C n -1°C
3. a 6°C up b 5°C down
   c 15°C down d 9°C up
   e 9°C down f 15°C up
   g 7°C down h 13°C down
   i 80°C up j 12°C down
4. -15°C
5. 44°C
6. 49°C
7. a 1°C b -3°C c -7°C d -31°C
8. a -21°C, -2°C, -1°C, 0°C, 1°C, 18°C
   b -58°C, -36°C, -17°C, -9°C, -2°C, 2°C,

Chapter 8 - Exercise 3 (page 84)

1. a 15 b 16 c 14 d 2
   e 7 f 0 g -3 h -6
   i -16 j 8 k 0 l 17
   m -6 n -8 o -9 p -22
   q -18 r -22 s -11 t -6
2. a 7 b 0 c 19 d -6
   e -5 f -10 g -25 h -8
   i -7 j -24 k -24 l -27
   m -20 n -41 o -300 p -200
3. a 13 b -4 c -10 d 10
   e -12 f -2 g -14 h -52
   i 15 j -46 k -17 l -23
   m 9 n -1 o 0 p -24
4. a 5 b 0 c 2 d -2
   e -20 f -14 g 4 h -1
   i -18 j -1 k -50 l -900
5. a 14 b 17 c -2 d -3
   e -20 f 3 g 0 h -3
   i -6 j 20 k 40 l -1000
6. a 8 b 5 c 11 d 4
   e 5 f 3 g 4 h -4

Answers to CHAPTER 9 (Page 87)

Chapter 9 - Exercise 1 (page 87)

1. a 6 miles b 12 miles
   c 200 miles d 6 miles
   e 45 miles f 1 mile
2. a 210 miles b 500 miles
   c 1520 miles d 30 miles
   e 330 miles f 160 miles
3. a 100 km b 360 km
   c 170 km d 6 km
   e 180 km f 50000 km
4. 1260 km
5. 60 miles

Chapter 9 - Exercise 2 (page 88)

1. a 4 hr b 3 hr c 4 hr d 10 hr
   e 3 hr f 9 secs g 3 hr h 4 hr
2. a 1.30 pm
   b 11.55 pm
   c 0210 next morning
3. a 1 hr b 2 hr c 2 hr d 5 hr
4. a 135 miles b 172 miles
5. a 3 hr b 3 hr d 4 hr
6. a 3 hr b 9.45 am
7. a 9 hr b 0630 Monday
8. a 5 hr b 7 hr c 11 hr d 15 hr

9. Cyprus, England, Japan, Hawaii, France, Cuba, United Arab Emirates, Australia.
10. Yes with 30 mins to spare
11. a two and a half hours
    b three and a half hours
    c two and a quarter hours

Chapter 9 - Exercise 3 (page 90)

1. a 3 mph b 10 mph c 30 mph
   d 50mph e 75 kph f 80 kph
2. a 8 kph b 80 kph c 10 metres per sec
   d 7 mps e 200 kph f 60 metres per min
3. a 90 mph b 364 kph c 68 mph
   d 4 mph e 13 mph f 15 mph
   g 75 mph h 430 mph i 3·5 mph
4. a 16 kph b 16 kph c 100 metres per min
   d 2 metres per min e 50 metres per min
   f 3 metres per sec g 0.5 metres per min
   h 30 metres per sec (or 30 mph)
5. 13 mph
6. a 3 hrs b 369 mph
7. 18 mph
8. (30 + 30) ÷ (2 + 3) = 12 mph
9. a 498 mph b 468 mph
   c 792 km/hr d 756 km/hr
10. South Africa, USA, Russia, USA, Cuba, Italy, Canada, China
11. a 12 km/hr b 6 km/hr
    c 800 km/hr d 80 words/min

Chapter 9 - Exercise 4 (page 92)

1. a 23 mph b 4 hr
   c 260 miles d 20 mph
   e 24 hr f 2156 miles
   g 8 hr
2. 157 km
3. 18 mph
4. 18 minutes
5. 560 km/hr
6. 9 hours
7. 64000 miles
8. a 154 metres per minute b 2 mins
9. 1880 miles
10. 20 minutes
11. a 3000 metres per hr b 50 m
12. a half a mile per hour
    b two and a half mph - 5 times as fast
13. a (20 02 2002) (01 02 2010), (11 02 2011) ...
    b (10 02 20 02 2001) (10 02 30 03 2001)
       (10 02 11 11 2001), ...

Answers to CHAPTER 10 (Page 96)

Consolidation of 2-D Work (page 96)

1. a hexagon b decagon
2. rectangle, isosceles triangle, equilateral triangle, pentagon, square, semi-circle
3. a scalene b equilateral
   c isosceles
4. a acute b right c obtuse
5. a obtuse angle isosceles triangle
   b right angle scalene triangle
   c acute angles isosceles triangle
6. 13 cm
7. see drawing

Chapter 10 - Exercise 1 (page 97)

1. a yes b yes c yes d 4
   e (i) yes (ii) yes f 8 g yes
   h yes i yes j yes
2. a various

3 a/b

```
     10 cm
  E ┌──────────┐ F
    │14·1 cm  14·1 cm│
10 cm│    ╳     │10 cm
    │14·1 cm  14·1 cm│
  H └──────────┘ G
     10 cm
```

4. a/b 9·9 cm
5. a/b 5·7 cm
6. a/b 7·8 cm
7 a sides are 6 cm b diags are 8·5 cm
8. a 16 cm² b 100 cm²
   c 6·25 cm² d about 32 cm²
9. a 7 cm b 28 cm
10. 135°

Chapter 10 - Exercise 2 (page 99)

1. a no b yes c yes d yes
   e 2 f (i) yes (ii) no
   g 4 h yes i yes
   j no k no
2. various
3.

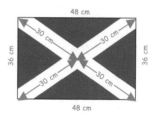

4. a/b 10 cm
5. various
6. various
7. a possibly 8 cm by 2 cm
   b possibly 7 cm by 3 cm
   c possibly 6 cm by 4 cm
   d a square
8. 21 cm²
9. a 120 cm² b 84 cm²
   c 70 cm²
10. 90cm²
11. a possibly 9 cm by 3 cm
    b 11 by 1, 10 by 2, 7 by 5, 6 by 6
    c 11 cm², 20 cm², 27 cm², 32 cm², 35 cm², 36 cm²
    d the one measuring 6 cm by 6 cm
    e a square - possibly always the square.

Chapter 10 - Exercise 3 (page 101)

1. a yes b yes c no d yes
   e 2 f (i) yes (ii) no g 4
   h no i yes j yes k yes
2. various
3. a 13 mm b 5 mm and 12 mm
4. see drawing
5. a/b 4·5 cm
6. see drawing
7. a see drawing b a square

Chapter 10 - Exercise 4 (page 102)

1. a no b no c yes d no
   e no f no g yes h 1
   i no j 2
2. a no b no c yes
   d yes e no f yes
3. various

4. a
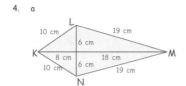
   b (i) KN   (ii) ML   (iii) ON
     (iv) NKO (v) KLO (vi) NMO
5. a Rhombus   b Square
6. 11 cm

Chapter 10 - Exercise 5 (page 104)

1. a no   b yes   c yes   d no
   e yes   f (i) yes (ii) no g 0
   h 2   i no   j yes
   k no   l no
2. various
3.
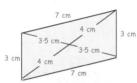
4. a rectangle (or square or rhombus)
   b rhombus (or square)
   c square

Chapter 10 - Exercise 6 (page 105)

1. square   2. rhombus
3. parallelogram   4. kite
5. rhombus   6. square
7. kite   8. rhombus
9. rectangle or parallelogram
10. kite   11. square
12. rhombus or parallelogram
13. rhombus   14. kite
15. square   16. rectangle
17. square   18. rectangle
19. kite   20. rectangle
21. rhombus   22. kite
23. parallelogram
24. it has 1 pair of parallel sides

25. various

Consolidation of Algebra Work (page 108)

1. a 3   b 8   c 4
2. a 5   b 6   c 30
   d 19   e 7   f 0
   g 9   h 5·1   i 55
3. a -   b x   c +
   d +   e ÷   f x
   g +   h -   i ÷
4. a 14   b 25   c 9
   d 14   e 30   f 11
5. a $* + 26 = 55$ b 29 km
6. a (i) 56 (ii) 14 b (i) 4 (ii) 35

Chapter 11 - Exercise 1 (page 109)

1. a (i) 5 (ii) 23 (iii) 53 (iv) 7·6 (v) 3
   b (i) 3 (ii) 12 (iii) 150 (iv) 3·3 (v) 9·4

2. a (i) 25 (ii) 34 (iii) 23·5 (iv) 118 (v) 0·4
   b (i) 6 (ii) 15 (iii) 12 (iv) 1·5 (v) 100
3. a 44   b 27   c 21
   d 30   e 8   f 0
   g 41   h 12
4. a 2   b 8
   c 14   d 9·5
5. a 16   b 8   c 8
   d 3   e 12   f 48
6. a 6   b x
   c 18   d ÷
7. various e.g. 100 ÷ 5 + 5 = 25, 100 - 95 x 5 = 25

Chapter 11 - Exercise 2 (page 111)

1. a 4   b 3   c 16
   d 10   e 9   f 22
   g 10   h 60   i 0
   j 18   k 15   l 80
   m 4   n 3   o 9
   p 35   q 3   r 0
   s 40   t 68   u 246
2. a 2   b 5   c 6
   d 4   e 6   f 10
   g 12   h 6   i 12
   j 11   k 14   l 9
   m 11   n 8   o 3
   p 2·5   q 4·5   r 9·5
   s 2·5   t 1·5   u 5·5
   v 5·25   w 3·4   x 4·8

Chapter 11 - Exercise 3 (page 112)

1. a 3   b 4   c 5
2. a 1   b 5   c 4
   d 8   e 5   f 9
   g 9   h 2   i 9
   j 10   k 3   l 7
   m 7   n 3   o 0
   p 20   q 1   r 2·5
   s 5   t 3·5   u 2·5
3. a $x + 8$ b (i) $x + 8 = 21$ (ii) $x = 13$
4. a $x + 8 = 17$ b $x = 9$ (£9)
5. a $x - 7 = 14$ b $x = 21$ (21 marbles)
6. a (i) $x + 14 = 31$ (ii) $x = 17$
   b (i) $y + 2·3 = 3·1$ (ii) $y = 0·8$
   c (i) $p + 20 = 34$ (ii) $p = 14$
7. a Area = $4 \times x \times b$ (i) $4x = 24$ (ii) $x = 6$
8. a 14   b 27   c 80
   d 50   e 50   f 16
   g 66   h 100   i 7
   j 10   k 18   l 12
   m 6   n 10   O 20

Chapter 11 - Exercise 4 (page 114)

1. a >   b <   c >
   d <   e >   f >
   g <   h <   i >
2. a 3 < 8   b 8 > 3   c 11 < 17
   d -5 > -8 e 2 > -2 f -1 < 5
   g -15 < -14 h -77 > -79 i -10 < 9
3. a 3,4   b 0,1,2,3   c 3,4
   d 0,1   e 1,2,3,4 f 0,1,2,3,4
   g --   h 0,1,2,3,4 i 0
4. a 2,3   b -3,-2,-1   c -1,0,1,2,3
   d -3,-2,-1,0,1 e -2,-1,0,1,2,3 f -3,-2
   g -1,0,1,2,3   h -3,-2,-1,0 i all
5. a $C ≤ 14000$ b (i) $Y ≥ 18$ (ii) $T < 18$
   c $P ≤ 51$ d $V > 20$ e $S ≤ 12$
   f $Y ≥ 6$ g $M ≥ 40$ h $P < 6$
   i $M ≥ 16$ j $T > 220$ k $x + y ≥ 40$

Chapter 11 - Exercise 5 (page 116)

1. a $x > 4$ b $x > 9$ c $x ≤ 1$

   d $x < 8$ e $x ≤ 9$ f $x ≥ 25$
   g $x > 10$ h $x < 70$ i $x ≤ 0$
   j $x ≥ 8$ k $x < 1$ l $x > 80$
   m $x < 1·1$ n $x > 210$ o $x < 1/2$
   p $x > 2$ q $x ≥ 7$ r $x < 4$
2. a $x < 7$ b $x > 5$ c $x < 11$
   d $x ≥ 9$ e $x ≤ 7$ f $x > 10$
   g $x < 5$ h $x ≤ 10$ i $x > 0$
   j $x ≥ 1$ k $x < 3$ l $x > 3$
   m $x > 2·3$ n $x ≤ 10$ o $x ≥ 100$
   p $x < 800$ q $x > 250$ r $x ≤ 24$
3. a $x + 120 > 190$, $x < 70$
   b $x + 400 > 775$, $x > 375$
   c $x - 10 > 35$, $x > 45$
   d $2x < 50$, $x < 25$
   e $2x > 60$, $x > 30$
4. a $x < 4$ b $x > 4$ c $x < 0$
   d $x ≥ 8$ e $x ≤ 24$ f $x > 11$
   g $x ≤ 1$ h $x < 3$ i $x > 6$
   j $x ≥ 6$ k $x < 5$ l $x ≤ 11$
   m $x ≥ 3$ n $x < 0$ o $x ≥ 2·5$
   p $x ≥ 30$ q $x < 0$ r $x ≥ 50$
5. a 4,5   b 1,2,3,4   c 0,1,2
   d 6,7   e 1,2,3   f -1,0,1,2,3
   g 1,2,3   h 2,3,4,5,6
   i 2,3   j -2,-1,0,1,2

Consolidation of Fractions/Decimals and Percentages (page 119)

1. a $3/7$ b $7/10$ c $5/8$
2. a $4/7$ b $3/10$ c $3/8$
3. a $5/20$ b $9/21$ c $13/15$
4. a $2/12$, $3/18$ b $10/16$, $15/24$ c $6/20$, $9/30$
5. a $1/3$ b $3/4$ c $2/3$
6. a £9   b 50 m   c $12
7. a 6   b 4   c £5·30
8. a £18   b $120   c £2100
9. 40
10. red 34%, blue 30%, green 14%, yellow 22%
11. a $21/100$ b $39/100$ c $11/100$ d $37/100$
    e $1/100$ f $9/100$ g $19/100$ h $25/100$
12. a 0·43 b 0·13 c 0·29 d 0·09
    e 0·05 f 0·50 g 1·25 h 0·01
13. a $17/100$, 0·17 b $69/100$, 0·69
    c $3/100$, 0·03 d $30/100$, 0·30
    e $70/100$, 0·70 f $50/100$, 0·50
    g $25/100$, 0·25 h $10/100$, 0·10
14. a 79% b 67% c 57% d 1%
    e 9% f 3% g 90% h 170%
15. a 15p b 9 mm c £7·50 d 70 cm
    e 250 g f £1·10 g 2·5 km h 27·5 cm
16. a £616   b 612 km
    c £148·20   d 21p
17. a (i) 12000 (ii) 3000 (iii) 5000
    b (i) 600 ft (ii) 900 ft

Chapter 12 - Exercise 1 (page 121)

1. a $1/4$ b $3/10$ c $3/20$ d $23/100$
   e $1/50$ f $9/100$ g $19/20$ h $3/4$
   i $1/20$ j $17/50$ k $33/50$ l $16/25$
   m $2/5$ n $3/5$ o $4/5$ p $27/100$
2. 40% = $2/5$, 50% = $1/2$, 5% = $1/20$, 75% = $3/4$,
   10% = $1/10$, 1% = $1/100$, 100% = 1, 25% = $1/4$
3. 1, $3/4$, $1/2$, $1/4$, $1/5$, $1/10$, $1/20$, $1/100$

4. a £12 b 50 kg c 30p d 1300km
5. a £8 b £9 c £8·20
    d 6 mm e $30 f £2·50
    g £30 h £1·20 i £600
6. a 0·8, $^{79}/_{100}$, 0·78, 77%
    b $^2/_5$, 0·3, $^8/_{31}$, 0·225, 22%
    c 29%, $^3/_{11}$, 0·24, $^2/_9$
    d $^4/_{11}$, $^1/_3$, $^3/_{10}$, $^2/_7$, $^7/_{26}$
7. a various b various
8. a best French - worst English
9. £3600, £4200, £3000 - best is (ii)

Chapter 12 - Exercise 2 (page 123)

1. Copy and Learn
2. a £12 b £24 c £48
    d £4 e £2 f £180
    g £5 h £10 i £35
    j £4·20 k £152 l £210
    m £3·10 n £6·20 o £1·50
    p £27 q £18 r £9
    s £7 t £14 u £21
    v £360 w £1300 x £6
    y £3 z £3·30
3. a 10% + half your answer
    b 10% halved and halved again
    c 10% + 5% + 2½% - added
4.   a £12 b 24 km
    c 35 km d 10p e 84 ml
    f £112 g £1·40 h 259 ml
    i 360 mm j 18 cm k 90 litres

Chapter 12 - Exercise 3 (page 124)

1. 42 pupils
2. 104 trees
3. 170 g
4. 38 cats
5. a £55 b (i) 17 kg (ii) 68 kg
    c £285 d (i) 90 (ii) 40%
    e 24
6. a £40 b £1710
7. a £105 b £42
8. a £896 b 4730
    c £67·20 d £4200
9. 69 mph
10. a £31·08 b £344·50 c 42 psi
11. a £102·30 b £11872
12. a £10000 b £200
    c £4000 d £10000

Consolidation of Measurement (page 127)

1. a 67 mm b 49 mm
2. a (i) 85 mm (ii) 8·5 cm (iii) 8 cm 5 mm
    b (i) 37 mm (ii) 3·7 cm (iii) 3 cm 7 mm
3. See drawing
4. a 300 cm b 120 mm c 1800 m
    d 6 km e 2·7 m f 12 cm
    g 4·7 km h 295 cm i 2020 cm
    j 350 cm k 117 mm l 6·05 m
5. 267 mm
6. 21·5 m
7. 7 cm
8. £38·00
9. a 28 cm² b 24 cm²
10. a see drawing b 18 boxes c 18 cm²
11. a 40 cm² b 49 m²
12. a 21 m² b £84·00
13. see drawing b 15 cm² c 7·5 cm²
14. 24 m²

15. teacup, jug, bucket, (barrel/bath)
16. lasts 20 weeks - ok
17. a 6 b 40
    c 3 d 14
18. a 650 ml
19. a 15 cm³ b 28 cm³
20. a (i) 6000 ml (ii) 13500 ml (iii) 800 ml
    b (i) 4·5 litres (ii) 25 litres (iii) 0·25 litre
21. 42 m³
22. grape, plum, apple, pineapple, watermelon
23. a 3000 g b 500 g c 16500 g
    d 1200 g e 5015 g g 2750 g
24. a 3 kg b 12·5 kg c 0·25 kg
    d 6·4 kg e 5·03 kg f 1·005 kg
25. a 350 g
26. 30 kg 600 g
27. 23 kg
28. 850 grams
29. 15 kg 213 g (15·213 kg)

Consolidation of Patterns (page 131)

1. a

2. a start at 8 and rise by 12 each time
    b 68, 80, 92, 104
3. a start at 97 and go down by 9 each time
    b 52, 43, 34, 25
4. a start at 8 and rise by 7 - 43, 50, 57, 64
    b start at 5 and rise by 18 - 77, 95, 113, 131
    c start at 83 and fall by 6 - 59, 53, 47, 41
    d start 1·8, rise by 2·5 - 14·3, 16·8, 19·3, 21·8
5. a M, P, S b P, N, L
6. a 4 rows of 4 topped by 4 rows of 3
    b 28 c 28, 35, 42, 49, 56
    d start at 7 and go up by 7 each time
7. a 1, 4, 9, 16, 25, 36, 49 b 400

Chapter 14 - Exercise 1 (page 132)

1. a

    b 3, 6, 9, 12, 15, 18 c 3
    d no. of children = 3 × no. of tables
    e C = 3 × T d 60
2. a

    b 5, 10, 15, 20, 25, 30 c 5
    d no. of circles = 5 × no. of stars
    e C = 5 × S f 200
3. a 6, 12, 18, 24, 30, 36 b 42
    c no. of strawberries = 6 × no. of glasses
    d S = 6 × G e 60
4. a 7, 14, 21, 28, 35, 42
    b cost = 7 × no. of footballs
    c C = 7 × F d £210
5. a no. of roses = 8 × no. of bushes
    b R = 8 × B c 400
6. a no. of marigolds = 10 × no. of pots
    b M = 10 × P c 150
7. a 14, 28, 42, 56, 70, 84
    b S = 14 × L, 280

8. a 20 b P = 20 × B c 360
9. a P = 30 × N b P = 18 × T
    c H = 24 × N d P = 100 × N
    e C = 1·25 × N f B = 150 × J
    g C = 3·5 × T

Chapter 14 - Exercise 2 (page 136)

1. a

    b 3, 5, 7, 9, 11, 13 c 2
    d C = 2 × S + 1 e 21
2. a

    b 8, 12, 16, 20, 24, 28 c 4
    d C = 4 × T + 4 e 84
3. a (i) £17 (ii) £20 b £3
    c C = 3 × D + 5 d £47
4. a 50 kg b 1450 kg
    c W = 50 × P + 1200 d 1700 kg
5. a

    b 4, 8, 12, 16, 20, 24 c 4
    d S = 4 × P - 4 e 76
6. a

    b 4, 7, 10, 13, 16, 19 c 3
    d C = 3 × T - 2 e 148
    f (i) 8 (ii) 12 (iii) 20 (iv) 30
7. a W = 3 × T + 7 b F = 5 × K - 3
    c B = 10 × F + 5 d G = 0·5 × C + 7
    e C = 4 × T + 8 f T = 6 × P + 24
    g C = 9 × D - 2 h D = 0·8 × T + 0·5
    i W = 60 × I + 180 j S = 250 × Y - 150
    k R = 23 - 3 × N

Consolidation of Coordinates (page 142)

1. a (i) P (ii) S (iii) V (iv) J
    b (i) (2,3) (ii) (0,5) (iii) (5,4) (iv) (7,7)
    c (i) RYTV (ii) (2,6), (8,6), (9,9), (3,9)
    d S e U f W
    g Q(2,3) h K, Z and T
2. a See drawing b D(5,8) c K(5,6)

Chapter 15 - Exercise 1 (page 143)

1. F(4, 4), G(5, 1), H(5, -2), I(6, -3),
    J(0, -2), K(-4, -3), L(-3, 0), M(-4, 2)
2. a kite b isosceles triangle
    c parallelogram d rhombus
    e hexagon f pentagon
3. a/b C(-2, -2) or C(7, 4)
4. a P(-2, 4), Q(-4, 2), R(-2, 0), S(0, 2)
    b P'(-2, -4), Q'(-4, -2), R'(-2, 0), S'(0, -2)
    c P''(2, -4), Q''(4, -2), R''(2, 0), S''(0, -2)
5. a/b parallelogram

c/d K'(-2, -2), L'(-3, 1), M'(3, 1), N'(4, -2)
6. a/b Pentagon
   c E'(-6,1), F'(-7,4), G'(-2,6), H'(3,4), I'(2,1)
   d E''(6,-1),F''(7,-4),G''(2,-6), H''(-3,-4),
      I' '(-2,-1)
7. a see diagram   b W(4, -3)
   c T(3, 4), U'(1, 6), V(-6, -1), W'(-4, -3)

Answers to CHAPTER 16 (Page 146)

Consolidation of 2-D Work (page 146)

1. a cylinder   b cone
   c cube   d hemisphere
   e sphere   f cuboid
   g pyramid   h triangular prism
2. a cube, cuboid and cone
   b cylinder cuboid and triangular prism
3. a 12   b 3   c 8   d 9
   e 5   f 0   g 1   h 5
   i 1   j 1
4. a square pyramid   b cylinder
5. see drawing

Chapter 16 - Exercise 1 (page 147)

1. Possible answer

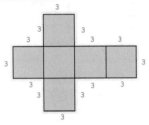

2. Possible answer

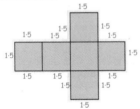

3. a yes   b no   c yes
   d no   e yes   f yes
4. various
5. a one above and 1 below the line of 4
   b never put both squares above or below.

Chapter 16 - Exercise 2 (page 149)

1. a/b

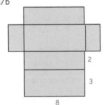

2. a/b

3. a/b/c see nets
4. a   b

5. a see nets and figures

Chapter 16 - Exercise 3 (page 150)

1.

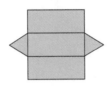

2.

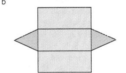

3. a 3 rectangles - 8 by 5, 8 by 5 and 8 by 3
   b

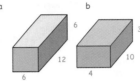

4.

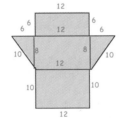

5. (i)   cube   (ii)   cuboid
   (iii) sphere   (iv)   cone
   (v)   cylinder   (vi)   square pyramid
   (vii) triangular prism (viii) hemisphere
   b A = cuboid   B = square pyramid
     C = cylinder   D = triangular prism
     E = cone   F = square prism
6. 336 cm²

Chapter 16 - Exercise 4 (page 152)

1. a/b   see model
2. a/b/c see models
3. a 192 cm   b 140 cm   c 155 cm
4. a see model   b 206 cm
5. a/b see model

Answers to CHAPTER 17 (Page 156)

Consolidation of Statistics (page 156)

1. a (i) 50 (ii) 115 (iii) 80 (iv) 35
   b 75   c going to work or school
   d few people start work at that time
   e people have already left for work.
2. a (i) 16 (ii) 28 (iii) 22 (iv) 18
   b balti (2)
   c nearly 4 times higher than tallest column
3. a see bar graph
4. a donuts - 8 , buns - 11, eclairs - 3
      apple pie - 3, muffins - 5
   b see graph
5. a 48   b Mon,Fri c 9
6. a (i) 125 (ii) 150
   b Sat   c 75
   d Thursday to Friday   e various
7. a see graph
   b bad weather possibly
8. a 200   b 100   c 50   d 50
9. a ¹/₂₀ b (i) ⁶/₂₀ (ii) ¹⁴/₂₀
   c (i) 60 (ii) 140
10. a 10%   b see drawing
11. a £850   b Fly Dubai
    c (i) Ryanjet (ii) June
12. a Mon   b Mon
    c (i) Feb 22nd (ii) Tue
    d (i) Jan 31st (ii) Mon
    e Frid 4th March   f Mon 17th January
    g Sunday   h Friday
13. a vertical scale does not start at zero
    b no indication of the name of the brand
    c the columns have varying widths

Answers to CHAPTER 18 (Page 160)

Chapter 18 - Exercise 1 (page 160)

1. a unlikely   b likely   c impossible
2. more losses
3. a unlikely   b an even chance
   c impossible d likely
4. likely

Chapter 18 - Exercise 2 (page 161)

1. a 1 in 2 (evens)
2. 1 in 3
3. 1 in 2 (evens)
4. 1 in 5
5. 1 in 8
6. 1 in 4
7. 6 in 12 or 1 in 2 (evens)
8. 6 in 9 or 2 in 3
9. a 1 in 3   b 1 in 2
   c 1 in 6   d 0
10. 3 in 12 or 1 in 4
11. 1 in 4
12. 1 in 4 - (H,H), (H,T), (T,H), (T,T)
13. a 1 in 36   b 1 in 9
    c 1 in 6   d 0

Answers to CHAPTER 19 (Page 164)

1. a 12000 b 36000
2. a 4700 + 1900 about 6600
3. a 10200 b 16700
4. a twenty thousand eight hundred and six
   b three million two hundred and seven
      thousand and eighty
5. a 3210 b 32258 c 10164 d 7538

6. a 15720 b 108630 c 1433 d 11292
7. a 447 g b 4500 ml c £4342 d 1375 mi
8. a 258 b 3·92 c 0·74
9. a 5017000 b 3308 c 96300 d 1600
10. 35
11. a 30 b 12·1 c 5·10 d 200·0
12. a 22·57 b 85·93 c 48·42 d 15·635
     e 62·39 f 22·24 g 3·95 h 105·28
13. a 60·301 b 0·236 c 234 d 0·068
14. a 4 b 38 c 2 d 24
15. -16°C
16. a -6 b 6 c -4 d -30
17. a 32, 36 b 53, 46 c 1, -1 d 16, 32
18. a 3, 6, 9, 12, 15, 18, 21, 24, 27, 30
     b 13, 26, 39, 52, 65, 78, 91, 104, 117, 130
19. a 1, 2, 3, 4, 6, 12 b 1, 2, 5, 10, 25, 50
20. 2, 3, 5, 7, 11, 13, 17, 19, 23, 29, 31, 37, 41,
     43, 47
21. $^1/_9$ 22. $^7/_{22}$ 23. 36% 24. 10%

25 a $^6/_{10}$ b $^{14}/_{22}$

26. a $^3/_4$ b $^2/_3$

27. a £1·60 b 150 m
28. 35%, $^2/_5$, 0·45

29. a $^{11}/_{20}$ b $^6/_{25}$

30. a £8 b 40p c 32·5p
31 80%
32. Yes since items come to £43·25
     I have £45, Left with £1·75
33. first is 12p per square, 2nd is 11p per square
34. $320 35. £14·50
36. a 3.50 pm b 12.10 am
37. a 2 min 5 secs b 325 mins
38. a 8 min 20 sec b 3 min 25 sec
39. Owens by 3·70 secs
40 7 hr 11 mins
41. a 70 km/hr b 24 km c 3 hr
42. about 1·8 to 2 metres
43. 19 cm^2
44. a 52 mm, 5·2 cm, 5 cm 2mm
     b 97 mm, 9·7 cm, 9 cm 7 mm
45. a 536 cm b 1004 cm
46. a 2·345 kg b 5·050 kg
47. a 3200 ml b 4750 ml
48. 3·65 km
49. a 15 m^2 b 6 cm^2
50. 8 cm
51. a 6000 cm^3 b 6 litres
52. $L = 6 \times H$
53. $W = 3 \times N + 5$
54. a 7 b 8 c 5
55. -1, 0, 1, 2, 3
56. various
57. 8
58. A = triangular prism, B = square pyramid
     C = cylinder D = cone
59. a acute b reflex
60. a 55° b 140°
61. North West
62. 070°
63. 84 cm
64. a A(9, 4) b B(5, 7)
65. a 30% b 90
66. 1 in 3
67. $^3/_{10}$
68. a b